Richard Harwood OBE QC specialises in planning, environmental, public and art law at 39 Essex Chambers. In particular he acts for art owners, regulators and third parties on the removal of works of art, listing, export control and contested heritage. His recent major heritage cases have included *Dill* in the Supreme Court and the Stonehenge road tunnel.

David Sawtell is at 39 Essex Chambers. He was called to the Bar by Lincoln's Inn in 2005. His practice combines property law, construction law and commercial work, both domestically and internationally. He undertook his BA and his MPhil at the University of Cambridge, and completed the MSc in Construction Law at King's College, London. David is a Fellow of the Chartered Institute of Arbitrators. He is currently researching towards his PhD at the University of Cambridge.

Catherine Dobson has a broad practice which combines general public law, environmental law and public international law. She has developed a niche expertise in historic environment matters, and has acted for owners and interest groups on art and antiquities matters, in particular on issues relating to the removal of art from historic buildings. She acted (led by Richard Harwood QC) for the successful for the former owner *in Dill v Secretary of State for Communities and Local Government* [2020] UKSC 20, where the Supreme Court clarified the test for what can constitute a listed building. She has recently advised on the lawfulness of removal of a high value statue from a listed building. She has lectured on these topics at the Institute of Art and Law and is a Fellow of St Edmund's College, Cambridge, where she teaches constitution law. In 2020 Catherine was named Environmental and Planning Law Junior of the Year in the Chambers UK Bar Awards.

Contested Heritage

Removing Art from Land and Historic Buildings

Contested Heritage

Removing Art from Land and Historic Buildings

Richard Harwood
Barrister, Middle Temple
OBE, QC, MA (Hons) (Cantab), LLM (Cantab)

David Sawtell
Barrister, Lincoln's Inn
MA (Hons) (Cantab), MPhil (Cantab),
MSc (King's College London), FCIArb

Catherine Dobson
Barrister, Inner Temple
MA (Hons) (Cantab), BCL

Law Brief Publishing

Published 2022 by Law Brief Publishing, an imprint of Law Brief Publishing Ltd
30 The Parks
Minehead
Somerset
TA24 8BT

www.lawbriefpublishing.com

Paperback: 978-1-914608-25-4

To the memory of Professor
Norman Palmer QC (Hon) CBE

ACKNOWLEDGEMENTS

The task of writing a book is made immeasurably easier by the time spent arguing, advising, discussing, researching and teaching on and around the issues over many years.

From Richard's perspective thanks are due in particular for involvement in cases, writing and seminars to Richard Aydon, Henrietta Billings, Catherine Croft, Marcus Dill, Nigel Hewitson, Emily Gould, Rebecca Hawkes-Reynolds, Alex Herman, Julia Rodrigues Casella Hommes, Antonia Layard, Joseph Mirwitch, Wendy Philips, Ruth Redmond-Cooper, Simon Stanion, Clarissa Vallat, Sheridan Westlake and Rupert Werff. The students on the Institute of Art and Law's diploma in art law courses and Queen Mary's Art, Business and Law LLM have also enriched the debate with their comments and contributions in seminars. Finally a debt is owed to the late Norman Palmer who suggested a long time ago that the removal of art from listed buildings was the topic of the day.

Catherine would like to thank Richard Harwood for introducing her to this fascinating area of law early in her career.

David is grateful to Professor Martin Dixon, for his encouragement and support during his PhD research in respect of annexation of objects to land; and to the students at Peterhouse. Cambridge and at the Department of Land Economy, University of Cambridge he has had the privilege to discuss these issues with in the course of their supervisions.

Thanks are also due to those who have managed to establish, explain and illuminate the law on the topic. For this book, as readers will soon discover, the guiding text is the 2020 judgment of Lord Carnwath JSC in *Dill v Secretary of State for Communities and Local Government* which gives clarity to a mass of cases on what is a building, what is a listed building, and the effect of hanging tapestries. The case was one of two heard by Robert Carnwath in his last week in the Supreme Court, the other being about the rating of cash machines in supermarkets. His influence though extends further, having been SAVE Britain's Heritage's favourite counsel before his appoint to the Bench.

This book was borne of an idea by Tim Kevan of Law Brief Publishing, an old friend who had caught a webinar we had done. At our publishers Garry Wright has helped to get the book over the line.

Thanks are due to our colleagues in 39 Essex Chambers and in particular our clerks in the Planning, Environment and Property Group, who also cover the Art and Cultural Property Team, Andy Poyser, Elliott Hurrell, Olly York and Charlie Quant.

We could not though do any of this without home support. Richard would like to thank Grainne, and Cathan, James and Sophie for everything, basically. David thanks his wife, Elizabeth, for her continued patience with his fascination with knotty issues of land law. Catherine thanks her husband, Zack, her son Ellis (who aged four predicted the outcome of the Supreme Court judgment in *Dill v Secretary of State for Communities and Local Government*) and Lila who was born as this work was finalised.

Law and policy in England, Wales and Northern Ireland is stated as at 18th April 2022.

Richard Harwood OBE QC
Catherine Dobson
David Sawtell
April 2022

CONTENTS

TABLE OF CASES

TABLE OF LEGISLATION

INTRODUCTION

The impetus for this book comes from two sources. The first is the demand of art owners and the art market for confidence in dealing with artworks associated with land and buildings. The second is recent rise in disputes about contested heritage, where public memorials to historic individuals are seen as contentious because of the individual's conduct or beliefs.

Whether an artwork was part of a building it was in, or land it was sited on, was an enduring part of many nineteenth century disputes between tenants for life and estates. Similarly disputes have arisen between tenants and landlords over which of the tenant's alterations become part of the land and which can be removed. The purchaser of a property will want to know what they are buying and might be aggrieved to find that the nice works they had their eye on have been taken away by the vendor. These disputes are not confined to history. Land law courses tend to start with a discussion of *Tower Hamlets LBC v Bromley LBC*,[1] a case from 2015 case about the ownership of a Henry Moore statue weighing 1.5 tonnes.

Ownership issues arise in less contentious situations. Sometimes a great house may be owned by a trust whilst the chattels are owned by the family. Or the house may have been given to the National Trust and possession of the chattels licensed to them. Are particular tapestries, pieces of sculpture and antiquities chattels or part of the house? Determining who still owns what will be vital in resolving inheritance tax liabilities and whether items can be donated in lieu of tax. The ownership issues arising from annexation to the land are addressed in Chapter 7, with improper dealing with such items – conversion – addressed in Chapter 8. Issues relating to sales are discussed in Chapter 9.

Control is not simply a matter of ownership and what is agreed between parties. Some artworks might contribute to the value of where they are and there may be a public interest in keeping them there. In general art

[1] [2015] EWHC 1954 (Ch).

can be moved within the UK without needing any approval from the government at all.[2] The export of artworks might need a licence.[3]

However artworks which are buildings or which are attached to buildings or the land might need government consent before they can be moved. There may be a need for listed building consent, planning permission, conservation area consent or scheduled monument consent (or a combination of these). Whether consent is required and the processes for applying are considered in Chapter 1 (listed buildings), Chapter 2 (planning permission) and Chapter 3 (scheduled monuments and conservation area consent). Chapter 4 considers the principles and tactics involved in deciding whether consent should be granted.

These regulatory consents are of vital importance. If consent is needed, it may be very hard to get, as artistic works which are part of the building may contribute to its interest. Whether items can be removed without, say, listed building consent will be vital to dealings with the items and, often, the property itself. In 2007 the Marquis of Bute, the former racing driver Johnny Bute, put up for sale Dumfries House in East Ayrshire and its contents. The eighteenth-century listed house was designed by Robert Adam and was surrounded by a large estate. However the value of the house and estate was dwarfed by the value of the Thomas Chippendale furniture which had been made for it and which was intended to be sold off separately.[4] Much furniture, such as tables, chairs and freestanding cabinets, will not conceivably be part of a building and so capable of being subject to listed building control. At Dumfries House there was considerable debate about the status of Chippendale items such as overmantels, pier glasses and pelmets. Ultimately the house and its contents, with the estate, were purchased following the intervention of

[2] An exception is the discovery of treasure, which is the property of the Crown or a franchisee: see Treasure Act 1996.

[3] See the Export Controls Act 2002, the Export of Objects of Cultural Interest (Control) Order 2003 and the statutory guidance in *Export Controls on Objects of Cultural Interest* (DCMS, 2015).

[4] See *The Herald* 'Sale of the century: Marquis of Bute aims to raise nearly £20m' (13th April 2007).

Prince Charles.[5] The price, £45 million, reflected views on which Chippendale items could have been sold separately and which were part of the listed building.

In 2009 the owner of Idlicote House sold two lead urns and the stone piers which they rested on at auction. He and the auctioneer were unaware that these had been added to the list of listed buildings in 1986. Years later the removal was discovered by the local planning authority who took listed building enforcement action. This culminated in the decision of the Supreme Court in *Dill v Secretary of State for Communities and Local Government*[6] in 2020. *Dill* established the tests for what is a listed building or part of it and what is building for planning purposes and forms much of the discussion in the book.

The removal of items without any necessary listed building or scheduled monument consent, or certain unauthorised demolition within conservation areas, is an immediate criminal offence. The return of items removed without authorisation, including without planning permission, can be required even if they have changed ownership. Where the removal of an object of historical, architectural or archaeological interest was a criminal offence then the item will be tainted under the Dealing in Cultural Objects (Offences) Act 2003.[7] It is then an offence to deal dishonestly with the object, knowing or believing it to be tainted.[8] Dealing includes any sale or other acquisition or disposal or export.[9] The Arts Council England, who oversee the export of cultural objects from the UK, will raise questions on export licence applications as to whether consents were required and obtained.

---

[5] *The Guardian* 'Prince saves jewel in Scots crown' (28th June 2007).

[6] [2020] UKSC 20, [2020] 1 WLR 2206.

[7] Dealing in Cultural Objects (Offences) Act 2003, s 2. See 'Dealing in Cultural Objects (Offences) Act 2003' (Richard Harwood) Art, Antiquity and Law (2003) Vol 8, issue 4 and generally, *Historic Environment Law* (Richard Harwood, 2012, Institute of Art and Law), chapter 17.

[8] Dealing in Cultural Objects (Offences) Act 2003, s. 1(2).

[9] Dealing in Cultural Objects (Offences) Act 2003, s. 3.

A separate system of controls applies to items removed from churches. The Church of England regime, which requires a faculty from the chancellor of the diocese is considered in Chapter 6. Whilst reflecting listed building control in many ways, it is important to have in mind that the faculty jurisdiction does apply to some works which are within but not physically attached to the church building and there is a distinctive, and more restrictive, approach to the retention of valuable treasures.

The significance of listed building issues for the owners of art has been well understood in the art market, certainly since the turn of the century. They are now attracting a wider significance.

The Black Lives Matter protests in 2020 brought the ownership and regulatory control of statues and other memorials to wider attention and significance. An element in the campaigning has been to remove symbols of approbation of historic individuals whose conduct is now seen to have been reprehensible. That debate was of course not entirely new. Statues of Confederate generals had been contentious in the United States for many years. There had been a long running campaign against the statue of Cecil Rhodes at Oriel College, Oxford.

Another long running debate had concerned the statue of, and various buildings and places named after, Edward Colston in Bristol. Colston had been a major local philanthropist, but had derived much of his wealth from active involvement in the Slave Trade. At the height of the Black Lives Matter protests the statue was pulled down by a crowd, daubed in paint and thrown into the harbour.

We look at some of the legal issues arising from the Colston statue in the case study at the end of this book, but the statue's forceable removal (justified or not) galvanised the debate about whether memorials should be removed, explained or protected, and in respect of whom. This debate on 'contested heritage' has continued.

The response of some institutions and local government was to draw up lists of memorials which were now said to be disreputable.[10] The response of the UK government was to institute a policy of 'retain and explain'.[11] If an individual's past needed qualifying then that should be by explanation rather than removal. This was incorporated into English planning policy in January 2021[12] and is now in the National Planning Policy Framework.[13]

Memorials are by their nature permanent. They are attached to buildings and land. Many have qualities and history of their own. The removal of some memorials and statues would need listed building consent. Others might need planning permission or no regulatory consent at all: there being a complex set of exemptions from the need for planning permission for small scale demolition and various permitted development rights for demolition or alterations to certain types of buildings.

The 'retain and explain' policy therefore faced two practical challenges: some removals might not need any form of regulatory consent at all, and in other cases contentious proposals might not come to the attention of the Minister.

Consequently a package of changes was introduced in 2021.[14] These applied planning control to various statues and memorials[15] and removed

---

[10] For example, London Borough of Camden https://news.camden.gov.uk/cross-party-review-group-to-examine-statues-monuments-and-place-names/; Mayor of London Open call for Commission for Diversity in the Public Realm members; London Borough of Lambeth, Public Debate On Slavery-Related Monuments And Street Names.

[11] See the Secretary of State for Digital, Culture, Media and Sport letter to national museums and galleries and other arm's length bodies, 22nd September 2020 and the Public Statues debate in the House of Commons on 25th September 2020 (Hansard, vol 680).

[12] Written Ministerial Statement, Planning and Heritage Update by Robert Jenrick MP, 18th January 2021, UIN HCWS 713.

[13] NPPF (2021), §198.

[14] Foreshadowed in the 18th January 2021 Written Ministerial Statement.

[15] Town and Country Planning (Demolition – Description of Buildings) Direction 2021.

permitted development rights,[16] meaning that planning applications would have to be made. Obligations on local planning authorities to notify Historic England and the Secretary of State of certain listed building[17] or planning applications[18] were changed so that contentious applications could be considered by Ministers.

One aspect of contested heritage has been the naming of streets and places after now contentious persons.[19] The legislation for changing street names is discussed in Chapter 5. It can fairly be said to be archaic and overdue for complete replacement.

Whether dealing with art for art's sake or as contested heritage, the property and regulatory legal issues and public policy associated with them are considerable and have been the subject of significant change in the last two years. We seek to explain the hows and whys in the chapters which follow.

---

[16] Town and Country Planning (General Permitted Development etc.) (England) (Amendment) Order 2021, amending the Town and Country Planning (General Permitted Development) (England) Order 1995.

[17] See Arrangements for Handling Heritage Applications – Notification to Historic England and National Amenity Societies and the Secretary of State (England) Direction 2021.

[18] Town and Country Planning (Consultation) (England) Direction 2021.

[19] For example, Sir John Hawkins Square in Plymouth and Black Boy Lane in Haringey.

PART ONE

REGULATORY CONSENTS

OVERVIEW

The purpose of Part 1 of this book is to explain the regulatory issues which may arise when moving or altering heritage assets. Heritage assets are defined broadly in the National Planning Policy Framework as "*a building, monument, site, place, area or landscape identified as having a degree of significance meriting consideration in planning decisions, because of its heritage interest*". This book is concerned only with tangible heritage assets and the questions that arise when consideration is given to their removal or alteration.

There are numerous different types of heritage asset which may be subject to a requirement to obtain regulatory consent for alteration or removal. Whilst the analysis in this book is of general application, it will focus on the following three types of heritage assets which commonly raise regulatory issues:

a. Assets which are part of larger structures, such as paintings or statues fixed inside or outside buildings, or plaques;

b. Statues on plinths;

c. Freestanding statues.

The following forms of regulatory control may arise:

a. The asset may be a listed building, or part of a listed building, and its removal or alteration might require listed building consent;

b. A need for planning permission may arise;

c. The asset may be in a conservation area, giving rise to a need for conservation area consent in Wales and Northern Ireland, or different planning rules in England;

d. Occasionally, scheduled monument consent may be required.

In Part 1, each of these regulatory regimes is considered in turn. The common structure for these chapters is:

(i) whether the particular consent is needed to remove the asset;

(ii) whether any automatic consents apply;

(iii) means of determining whether consent should be applied for;

(iv) the process of applying for consent;

(v) the role of Ministers, including appeals.

The final chapter in Part I considers the issues which may arise when determining whether to grant regulatory consent, including the relevance of policy, as well as practical guidance. Certain heritage assets have generated controversy due to their association with historical iniquities. This is particularly the case in respect of statues and memorials to historical figures or events associated with the slave trade. In such situations there are sometimes calls to remove or alter the statue or monument. The final chapter of Part I concludes with consideration of how these issues may be relevant to the determination of applications for regulatory consent.

CHAPTER ONE

LISTED BUILDING CONSENT

Listed buildings are buildings placed on a national list because they are of special architectural or historic interest. The demolition of such buildings, or works to them which affect their special interest, require listed building consent. When considering the removal or alteration of a heritage asset, it is necessary to determine whether listed building consent is required. There are three questions to consider:

a. Is the asset listed as a building in its own right?

b. If the asset is not listed in its own right, is it part of a listed building?

c. If the asset is listed, whether in its own right or as part of a listed building, does the proposed work require listed building consent?

The listed buildings regime

The Secretary of State or Welsh Ministers are under a duty to list buildings of special architectural or historic interest under s. 1 of the Planning (Listed Buildings and Conservation Areas) Act 1990 ("the Listed Buildings Act 1990"):

> *"For the purposes of this Act and with a view to the guidance of local planning authorities in the performance of their functions under this Act and the principal Act in relation to buildings of special architectural or historic interest, the Secretary of State shall compile lists of such buildings, or approve, with or without modifications, such lists compiled by [Historic England] or by other persons or bodies of persons, and may amend any list so compiled or approved."*

The Department for Communities has this responsibility in Northern Ireland.[20] The decision to list a building may take into account:[21]

> *"(a) any respect in which its exterior contributes to the architectural or historic interest of any group of buildings of which it forms part; and*
>
> *(b) the desirability of preserving, on the ground of its architectural or historic interest, any feature of the building consisting of a manmade object or structure fixed to the building or forming part of the land and comprised within the curtilage of the building."*

Listed building consent is required for "*works for the demolition of a listed building or for its alteration or extension in any manner which would affect its character as a building of special architectural or historic interest*".[22]

Is a heritage asset listed as a building in its own right?

Section 1(5) of the Listed Buildings Act 1990 provides the definition of 'listed building':[23]

> *"In this Act "listed building" means a building which is for the time being included in a list compiled or approved by the Secretary of State under this section; and for the purposes of this Act—*
>
> *(a) any object or structure fixed to the building;*

---

[20] Planning Act (Northern Ireland) 2011, s. 80(1),

[21] Listed Buildings Act 1990, s. 1(3); Planning Act (Northern Ireland) 2011, s. 80(2)(b) .

[22] Listed Buildings Act 1990, s. 7(1); Planning Act (Northern Ireland) 2011, s. 85(1).

[23] In Wales, ss. (5A) does not apply and there is no equivalent of it in Northern Ireland. In Northern Ireland the curtilage date under paragraph (b) is "*before 1st October 1973*" but otherwise is the same as the Welsh provision: Planning Act (Northern Ireland) 2011, s. 80(7).

> *(b) any object or structure within the curtilage of the building which, although not fixed to the building, forms part of the land and has done so since before 1st July 1948,*
>
> *shall, subject to subsection (5A)(a), be treated as part of the building."*

There are two parts to the definition of a listed building: first, a building included in a list, so whatever building is in the list entry; and, secondly, the extended definition covering "*objects or structures*" which are fixed to the building or are part of the land, within the curtilage of the listed building. In the English provisions, subsection (5A)(a) provides for items within the extended definition or which do not contribute to special interest to be omitted from the list. The application of the extended definition is considered further in the section below.

What is 'on the list'

The starting point is to consider whether the heritage asset is listed in its own right. That task is aided by the fact that Historic England maintains a searchable electronic database as the National Heritage List for England.[24] The maps for older listings on the online database are not definitive and the original list entry may need to be checked in cases of doubt. This should be held by Historic England. Additionally a copy of the list entry will be a local land charge and so should be searchable at the local authority.[25] Cadw maintain the online Cof Cymru – National Historic Assets of Wales. The Historic Environment Record of Northern Ireland is kept in three online formats: the Northern Ireland Buildings Database; the Northern Ireland Sites and Monuments Record; and containing all in a map form, the Historic Environment Map Viewer.

---

[24] This is available online at https://historicengland.org.uk/listing/the-list/ . Also of assistance is the Heritage Gateway, which enables searches for information on England's historic sites and buildings, including images of listed buildings: available online at https://www.heritagegateway.org.uk/gateway/.

[25] Listed Buildings Act 1990, s. 2(2).

The list entry is to be interpreted from all the information available on the list. For example a building might be identified as listed even though the entry contains the wrong building name and street name.[26]

It is possible to list part of a building[27] so list entries sometimes need to be read with care. However an entry which simply identifies a building by name or number will usually refer to the whole building.

Since 2013 English list entries have been able, under s. 1(5A), to provide:

> *"(a) that an object or structure mentioned in subsection (5)(a) or (b) is not to be treated as part of the building for the purposes of this Act;*
>
> *(b) that any part or feature of the building is not of special architectural or historic interest."*

What is a building?

If the heritage asset does appear on the list of listed buildings, that may not be determinative of the matter. An issue may arise as to whether the item is in law capable of being a building for the purposes of s.1(5) of the Listed Buildings Act 1990. By s. 91(2), except where the context otherwise requires, "building" has the same meaning as in s.336 of the Town and Country Planning Act 1990 ("TCPA"), which provides:[28]

> *"'Building' includes any structure or erection, and any part of a building, as so defined, but does not include plant or machinery comprised in a building ..."*

The inclusion of "*structure or erection*" broadens building from its ordinary definition of a house or other structure with a roof and walls. Beyond widening the meaning of building, neither of those terms are particularly useful to applying the definition in practice. The question

26 *Barratt v. Ashford Borough Council* [2011] EWCA Civ 27, [2011] 1 P & CR 21.

27 *Shimizu Ltd v. Westminster City Council* [1997] 1 WLR 168 at 180 *per* Lord Hope of Craighead.

28 The same definition is in Planning Act (Northern Ireland) 2011, s.250(1).

therefore arises how to determine whether some is capable of being a building for the purposes of s.1(5) of the Listed Buildings Act 1990.

This issue was ruled upon by the Supreme Court in *Dill v Secretary of State for Communities and Local Government ("Dill")*.[29] The case concerned a pair of early 18th century lead urns (or finials), attributed to the Flemish sculptor John van Nost, each resting on a limestone pier from the 1720s. The piers were of a slab rather than solid construction. Together a pier and urn measured 274 cm high. The items were originally at Wrest Park but were subsequently moved several times before being placed either side of the driveway at Idlicote House in 1973. No alteration was made to the garden design to accommodate the items. The items were free-standing. The piers rested on concrete slabs and the urns were not attached to the piers.

Idlicote House had been made a listed building in 1966. In 1986 each set of urns and piers were made separate listed buildings. In 2009 Marcus Dill, who had inherited the items and was unaware that they had been listed, sold them at auction. In 2016, having been made aware of their removal, the local planning authority refused listed building consent for their removal and issued a listed building enforcement notice requiring their return. Mr Dill appealed to the Secretary of State on various grounds including that the items were not buildings and so were not listed buildings.

The Supreme Court agreed with Mr Dill that if the items were not buildings then listed building consent was not required for their removal, notwithstanding the fact that the items appeared on the list.[30] The

---

[29] [2020] UKSC 20, [2020] 1 WLR 2206.

[30] It had been argued on behalf of the Secretary of State that the fact that the items were on the list was determinative of the status of the subject matter as a listed building. This had been accepted by the High Court and the Court of Appeal: see Court of Appeal ([2018] EWCA Civ 2619; [2019] PTSR 1214) at §33. The Supreme Court rejected this submission stating, at §24: "*A listed building means "a building which is … included in [the] list …". Thus there are two essential elements: it must be both a "building" and it must be "included in [the] list …". If it is not in truth a building at all, there is nothing to say that mere inclusion in the list will make it so. […] There is nothing to prevent the accused arguing that the item on the list is not a "building" and so not within the definition.*"

Supreme Court did not determine whether the items were buildings or not, finding that was a matter for the Inspector or minister on redetermination of the appeal, but ruled on how the issue was to be approached as a matter of law.

The Supreme Court held that whether something is capable of being a building for the purposes of s.1(5) of the Listed Buildings Act 1990 should be approached in the same way as it is in planning law – applying the test from *Skerritts of Nottingham v Secretary of State for the Environment, Transport and the Regions (No.2)* ("*Skerritts*").[31] In *Skerritts*, whether a very large marquee[32] was a building was said to be judged by considering its size, permanence and degree of physical attachment.

Lord Carnwath JSC applied this approach in *Dill*, stating:[33]

> *"Given that the same definition of "building" is adopted in the Listed Building Act, it is difficult to see any reason in principle why the same test should not apply. On the other hand, notwithstanding the apparent width of the statutory definition, the mere fact that something had been "erected" on land was not sufficient to make it a building."*

How the *Skerritts* test will apply to statues, memorials and other heritage assets will depend on the facts of a particular case. There is limited assistance in the cases as to how the buildings test will be applied in practice to heritage assets. The planning cases have usually concerned large structures which involve assembly from multiple components: see, for example, the marquee in *Skerritts*, 39 hectares of polytunnels in *Hall Hunter Partnership v First Secretary of State*[34] and mobile poultry units

---

[31] [2000] JPL 1025.

[32] The Planning Inspector had said "*The marquee is a substantial object which is about 40m long, including the additions, and some 17m wide and the ridge height is around 5m … There is no direct evidence before me of the assembly method or period, but from my inspection, I consider that it took several days with a number of erectors and amounted to a sizable and protracted event*": see *Dill* at § 51.

[33] *Dill* at § 52.

[34] [2006] EWHC 3482 (Admin), [2007] JPL 1023.

being 20m x 6m x 3.5 metres in height in *R (Save Woolley Valley) v Bath and North East Somerset Council.*[35]

Some guidance is, however, provided in the judgment of Lord Carnwath in *Dill.* As noted above, the Supreme Court considered that whether the items were buildings was a matter for the Inspector or minister on the redetermination of the appeal, provided it was judged in accordance with law, rather than for the Court. They declined therefore to express a view on the status of the urns and piers. However, Lord Carnwath made the following observations about the arguments which could be applied to the urns and piers:[36]

> *"On the one hand, it can be said, they comprised a set of elements which had to be assembled together (a "structure"), required a small crane to move them and to assemble them (as an "erection"), and were intended to occupy a stable and near permanent position in situ (with greater permanence than the marquee in Skerritts). On the other hand, they are not particularly large, compared for example with the items considered in the three planning cases. It may also be relevant that the vases themselves, which are the real focus of the special interest, are physically separate. If they had been resting on the ground, rather than a plinth, I doubt if it would have occurred to anyone that they might qualify as buildings. Relevant also is the apparent ease of their installation and removal (as compared for example to the works in Skerritts)."*

In addition to the three factors referred to in *Skerritts*, Lord Carnwath also emphasised the importance of the means of erection and the need in the planning context for something akin to a building operation.[37] This is because the planning case law on whether structures are buildings has focused on this issue.[38] Since listed building consent concerned "*works*

[35] [2012] EWHC 2161 (Admin), [2013] Env LR 8.

[36] *Dill* at §58.

[37] *Dill* at § 52, § 53.

[38] See *Hall Hunter Partnership v First Secretary of State* [2006] EWHC 3482 (Admin), [2007] JPL 1023 and *R (Save Woolley Valley) v Bath and North East Somerset Council* [2012] EWHC 2161 (Admin), [2013] Env LR 8.

for the demolition" this "*clearly envisages some form of dismantling (ie "pulling down or taking to pieces" in the words of Jenkins J in the Cardiff case*[39]*) when the item is removed from the site*".[40] That is of some significance in considering whether a freestanding statue is a building, as a statue will often be capable of being removed in one piece. However a plinth will often be formed of stone or brick cemented together, and may be incapable of being moved intact. Where a statue is mounted on a plinth, then it might be case that the plinth is a building, but the statue is not, or there needs to be consideration as to whether the statue is fixed to the building[41], an issue considered in the following section.

Lord Carnwath also considered various examples given in Historic England's *Garden and Park Structures—Listing Selection Guide* ("*Selection Guide*").[42] Of Henry Moore's Reclining Woman (1947), at Dartington Hall, a large stone sculpture resting on a substantial stone base, listed Grade II, Lord Carnwath said "*even if the Dartington statue is resting by its own weight, the plinth appears as a substantial built structure, and together they appear to form an integral design for the site in which it is placed*".[43] These three factors were indicative that the sculpture could be a listed building in its own right. Similarly the group of 27 life-size Crystal Palace dinosaurs (listed Grade I), survivors from an exceptional High Victorian pleasure ground created in the early 1850s, "*having regard to their relative size and permanence (whether or not physically attached to the land) could reasonably have been seen as buildings in their own right*".

Another example from the *Selection Guide* was Wrest Park, the original site of the urns and plinths that were the subject of litigation in *Dill*. The Wrest Park gardens are given, in the *Selection Guide*, as an example of the reversion to the "*severely formal fashions of the seventeenth and earlier eighteenth centuries with terraces, balustrades, vases, basins and fountains, elaborate steps and gateways, seats, summerhouses, and statuary.*" Various

---

[39] *Cardiff Rating Authority v Guest Keen Baldwin's Iron and Steel Co Ltd* [1949] 1 KB 385.

[40] *Dill* at § 53

[41] See Listed Buildings Act 1990, s. 1(5)(a).

[42] *Dill* at §§ 30-32.

[43] *Dill* at § 56.

large classical statues, which were not fixed in place other than by their own weight but formed an intrinsic part of the design of the garden, were separately listed as "*buildings*" in their own right. The *Selection Guide* also referred to statuary, urns and other features such as sundials and astronomical devices, stating that pre-1850 examples will generally merit listing, even when they have been moved from elsewhere.[44] Lord Carnwath described this example in the *Selection Guide* as "*debatable*", stating:[45]

> *"It is hard to see how it could be appropriate to include without discrimination items such as "vases, basins … seats … and statuary", without any indication of how they might be brought within any part of the definition, whether as separate buildings or as curtilage structures under the extended definition. In particular, most ordinary forms of garden vases or seats would be unlikely to have become part of the land in real property terms, nor would they naturally be regarded as "buildings" under any of the tests considered above."*

In his consideration of examples provided in the *Selection Guide*, Lord Carnwath appears to have focused on the permanence of the heritage assets. Size was one indication of permanence, the larger the item the less likely it would be moved frequently or at all. Integration into the design was another. The Crystal Palace dinosaurs were central features of the pleasure ground and Moore's Reclining Woman was integral to the design of the Dartington Hall gardens. By contrast, the urns and piers in *Dill* had always been in private gardens and had been moved around between properties. This undermines their permanence, even though they were not moved regularly. This is not to say that public statues or memorials are always intended to be permanently sited. The permanence of items on a temporary display (such as artworks placed on Trafalgar Square's fourth plinth) or items on a long-term loan may be viewed differently. As the Supreme Court in *Dill* emphasised, how the *Skerritts* test will apply to statues, memorials and other heritage assets will depend on the facts of a particular case.

---

[44] *Dill* § 30.

[45] *Dill* at §56.

Is a heritage asset part of a listed building?

A heritage asset may be treated as part of a listed building under the extended definition of building provided by s.1(5) of the Listed Buildings Act 1990. There are two parts to the extended definition.

Objects or structures which are fixed to the listed building or part of the land

If the curtilage provision does not apply because the item was placed in its location after 1 July 1948, the question is whether the item is an "*object or structure*" which is "*fixed*" to the listed building or "*part of the land*" within the meaning of s.1(5)(a).

The meaning of "*object or structure*" has had limited judicial consideration, albeit on two occasions in the highest court. In *Debenhams plc v Westminster City Council* ("*Debenhams*"),[46] the House of Lords considered the meaning of "*object or structure*" for the purposes of a predecessor provision – s.54(9) of the Town and Country Planning Act 1971.[47] The issue in that case was whether or not a building adjoining a listed building was a structured fixed to that building. The listed building – formerly the site of Hamley's toy shop on Regent Street – was adjoined to a second building on Kingly Street by a footbridge passing over Kingly Street and a tunnel passing underneath it. Lord Keith, with whom Lords Templeman, Griffiths and Mackay agreed, stated that whilst the word "*structure*" in s.54(9) would in its ordinary significance cover any building, the word had a narrower meaning in the context to s.54(9). A wider meaning could lead to "*strange results*"[48]:

> "*For example, if one house in an architecturally undistinguished terrace were listed as having once been the birthplace of an historically famous personage, it appears that all the houses in the terrace, being*

---

[46] [1987] AC 396 at pp. 408-409.

[47] S.54(9) of the 1971 Act provided: "*for the purposes of the provisions of this Act relating to listed buildings and building preservation notices, any object or structure fixed to a building, or forming part of the land and comprised within the curtilage of a building, shall be treated as part of the building*".

[48] *Debenhams* at pp. 402G-H per Lord Keith of Kinkel.

> *fixed to the listed building either directly or through each other, would require to be treated as part of it, as indeed might many other terraces connected to that one. Many other such examples may be figured."*

He further held that the word "*structure*" was intended to convey "*limitation to such structures as are ancillary to the listed building itself, for example the stable block of a mansion house, or the steading of a farmhouse, either fixed to the main building or within its curtilage*".[49]

The meaning of "*fixed*" had first been addressed in the listing building context in *Corthorn Land and Timber Co Ltd v Minister of Housing and Local Government*[50] concerning whether various items inside a building were part of the building (prior to the introduction of the extended definition). Russell LJ applied the property law approach to fixtures to determine whether the items were part of a building for the purposes of a building preservation order, finding that they were.[51] In *Debenhams*[52] Lord Mackay of Clashfern explained, *obiter*, that "*fixed*" in what is now section 1(5)(a) had the property law meaning.

The Supreme Court in *Dill* confirmed that whether a structure or object is fixed or is part of the land under the extended definition in s.1(5)(a) is judged by application of the two-stage test derived from property law: (1) the method and degree of annexation and (2) the purpose of annexation.[53]

Property law, as a matter of private law, has needed to deal with the status of items in buildings and gardens in a variety of contexts: for example, what was included in the sale of a property; whether tenants could remove items they had fixed; whether items were bound by charges; the

---

[49] *Debenhams* at pp. 403F – G per Lord Keith of Kinkel.

[50] (1965) 17 P & CR 210.

[51] A building preservation order would prohibit the demolition, alteration or extension of a building in specified ways: Town and Country Planning Act 1962, s 30. At this time listing merely required notice to be given of some works, rather than requiring consent for works.

[52] At pp. 408-409.

[53] See *Dill* at § 36.

passing of property under a will. This was the issue that arose in *Berkley v Poulett,*[54] which concerned whether artworks should pass on as fixtures on the sale of a house. Scarman LJ said:[55]

> *"The answer today to the question whether objects which were originally chattels have become fixtures, that is to say part of the freehold, depends upon the application of two tests: (1) the method and degree of annexation; (2) the object and purpose of the annexation."*

Of particular relevance to the present context, the Court of Appeal held, by a majority, that a statue of a Greek athlete was not part of the land, although the plinth on which it rested was.[56] In *Tower Hamlets London Borough Council v Bromley London Borough Council* ("*Tower Hamlets*") [57] – a case concerning a Henry Moore bronze sculpture "Draped Seated Women" (nicknamed as "Old Flo") which had been placed in a new housing estate, the High Court held that it remained a chattel rather than part of the land.[58] Norris J concluded that Old Flo was not a fixture, in essence because it rested on its own weight (albeit weighing a considerable 1,500kg), could be removed with damage and was not in any sense dependent on the location for its appreciation. In the view of Norris J, "*the sculpture's power was no greater in Stepney than in Cologne or Melbourne*"[59].

Government guidance had recognised the use of the property law tests to determine what is a fixed to a listed building.[60]

---

[54] [1977] 1 EGLR 86.

[55] *Berkley* at p. 88.

[56] *Berkley* at p. 89.

[57] [2015] EWHC 1954 (Admin), [2015] LGR 622.

[58] *Tower Hamlets* at § 17 per Norris J. The property law cases are considered in more detail in the Annexation Chapter 7 below.

[59] *Tower Hamlets*, at § 17.

[60] *Planning Practice Guidance Note 15,* § 3.31 (cancelled in 2010); *Criteria for the Scheduling of Historic Monuments and the Listing of Buildings of Special Architectural or Historic Interest, with associated procedures* (Northern Ireland Department for Communities Historic Environment Division, May 2019), para 18.3.

<u>*Listing cases*</u>

A series of court, ministerial and inspector decisions have considered the application of the planning law and property law tests in a listed building context.

Scarisbrick Hall – Corthorn

In *Corthorn*[61] various portrait panels, wooden panels, a large wood carving of the Crowning with Thorns, and large wooden equestrian figures of St George and the Dragon and St Martin were inside the Nineteenth Century Scarisbrick Hall. The Court concluded that they were fixtures in property law terms, focussing on the method of fixing, albeit mentioning that "*each of the items in its particular place and setting was an integral and vital part of the whole architectural scheme of [Augustus] Pugin*". Russell LJ, siting in the High Court, held that any right of tenants to remove fixtures did not apply to the statutory meaning of building.

The Idlicote Hall urns – Dill

In *Dill*, the Supreme Court confirmed that the property law tests apply to determine whether an item is fixed to a building for the purposes of s.1(5)(a). Although not in issue in the case, Lord Carnwath considered the application of the real property law tests to the piers and urns. He concluded that tests would not have been satisfied, stating:[62]

> *"being freely movable, there is no suggestion that they were related in any relevant way to the design of that particular listed building and its setting. The applicable real property tests were not satisfied."*

Prior to its confirmation in *Dill* the property law approach had been followed and applied to various items inside buildings by the High Court, the Minister and Inspectors.

Three Graces at Woburn Abbey

61 (1965) 17 P & CR 210.

62 *Dill* at § 57.

Following the instigation of High Court proceedings by SAVE Britain's Heritage, the Secretary of State reconsidered whether the statue of The Three Graces by Canova were part of the listed Woburn Abbey. [63] The statue was commissioned by the 6th Duke of Bedford in 1816 and part of an existing gallery was remodelled (as the Temple of the Graces or the tempietto) to accommodate it. The statue was placed into recesses in a separately designed plinth. Whilst the plinth was screwed or bolted to the floor, but easy to remove, the statue was freestanding. The Minister attached importance to the following:

> *"(a) the Three Graces was expressly commissioned by the 6th Duke from a sculptor of prominence and has always been regarded as a major work of art;*
>
> *(b) the statue appears to have been commissioned before steps were taken to add the tempietto to the gallery;*
>
> *(c) the tempietto formed part of the gallery which was being converted and added to by the 6th Duke for the display or exhibition of sculpture;*
>
> *(d) the relative importance of the statue in its own right and the nature and character of the building;*
>
> *(e) the unlikelihood that sculpture put in a gallery for display is intended to become part of the building;*
>
> *(f) the probability that it was the tempietto which was designed to display or "show off" the statue rather than the statue which was commissioned and installed as part of the architectural design of the building;*
>
> *(g) the physical nature and degree of annexation."*

The Minister doubted whether the degree of physical annexation was sufficient but concluded in any event that it failed the purpose test: "*the object or purpose of installing the statue in the tempietto was not to dedicate it to the land or to incorporate it into the land, but to show off the statue*".

[63] The Secretary of State's decision is summarised at [1991] JPL 401.

This chattel status was consistent with the historic handling of the statue by the owners and revenue authorities.[64]

Leighton Hall – Kennedy

In *R v Secretary of State for Wales ex p Kennedy*[65] it was common ground that the fixture tests, as discussed in *Berkley v Poulett*, applied to the meaning of "*fixed*" in s. 1(5)(a). The High Court upheld as lawful the Secretary of State's view that carillon clock "*weighing many tons*" was fixed to the listed Leighton Hall. A challenge to the Secretary of State's finding that three bronze chandeliers hanging in the great hall were also part of the building had been abandoned.

Time and Life Building

In *Time and Life Building*, Westminster City Council had served listed building enforcement notices requiring the reinstatement of a Henry Moore bronze *Draped Reclining Figure*, a Ben Nicholson painting *Spirit of Architecture*, a Christopher Ironside clock *Astrolabe* and a Geoffrey Clarke sculpture *The Complexities of Man* in the Time and Life Building, New Bond Street. The building had been constructed in the early 1950s and listed grade II in 1988. On appeal the Inspector considered the purpose of annexation test at the date of listing rather than construction and quashed the notices.[66] The Council appealed to the High Court and the inspector's decision was quashed by consent. On re-determination, the Secretary of State considered that all the objects were fixtures having regard to the degree of annexation and the fact that all the works were

[64] Following further litigation over export licensing and grants (*R v Secretary of State for National Heritage ex p J Paul Getty Trust* (Court of Appeal, 27 October 1994), the statue was acquired by the National Galleries of Scotland and the V&A and remains in the UK: see *SAVE Britain's Heritage 1975-2005: Thirty Years of Campaigning* (Marcus Binney), pp 174, 175.

[65] *R v Secretary of State for Wales ex p Kennedy* [1996] 1 PLR 97 at 98-99 per Ognall J. The Secretary of State's decision letter is reported in part at [1995] JPL 256 and discussed by Gareth W Thomas in *Fixture or fitting? – the case of Leighton Hall, Montgomeryshire* [1995] JPL 187.

[66] [1995] JPL 241.

specifically designed to fit into particular spaces as part of an overall architectural design.[67]

Noseley Hall

In the *Noseley Hall*[68] case, the Secretary of State considered listed building enforcement notices against the removal of seven paintings of Roman ruins by followers of Giovanni Paolo Pannini from the study and two paintings of a hose, Ring Tail, from the Stone Hall. The property law tests were applied, as set out in *Berkley v Poulett*. One Pannini appeared to have been acquired in Italy and was in an overmantel, whilst the six smaller ones fitted over the six doors in the study and appeared to have been painted later, in England. In the Inspector's view, with which the Minister agreed:[69]

> *"the end result was a carefully conceived room based on the Early Georgian Classical principles of architecture adorned with seven paintings showing Classical Roman antiquities in idealised landscapes. The Appellants' witness described the architectural treatment of the chimney breast, ceiling and panelled walls as a complete entity. The single subject matter of the paintings reflecting the centrepiece Pannini, their uniformity in size and their close match with the dimensions of the door panels indicates to me that the design of the study was conceived as a whole and was intended to incorporate the seven paintings."*

Consequently "*the purpose was to enhance the beauty of the study by the careful matching of pictures with the interior architecture*" and the Panninis were part of the building.[70] Conversely the paintings of one of the 7th Baronet's favourite horses filled spaces in the hall, and their assimilation into the hall was well-mannered but slight in terms of the design. They

[67] Appeal reference APP/F/93/x5590/630150-1,[1999] JPL 292.

[68] Appeal reference APP/F2425/F/98/1012066, Noseley Hall, Noseley, Leicestershire, [1999] JPL 1145. (2000) V Art Antiquity and Law 37.

[69] Noseley Hall, Inspector's report, para 7.10.

[70] Inspector's report, para 7.12.

were not installed for the purpose of creating a beautiful room as a whole and were therefore not part of the building.[71]

The Kirkleatham Chandelier

A chandelier was held to be fixed to the listed Kirkleatham chapel in which it hung in an Inspector's appeal decision .[72] Applying the two tests, the Inspector considered that the chain and pulley system for the chandelier was part of one fixture giving a significant degree of annexation. On the object and purpose of annexation he held "*although the chandelier can be enjoyed as a work of craftsmanship, its object and purpose is not simply to make the chapel more attractive (which for reasons I set out below is in itself arguable), but with its mechanisms has been placed in the chapel to light it in specific way*".[73]

<u>*Objects or structures within the curtilage of a listed building*</u>

The second part of the extended definition applies to "*objects or structures*" which have formed part of the land within the curtilage of a listed building since before 1 July 1948.[74] If the object or structure is ancillary to the listed building then it will be covered by the listing pursuant to s.1(5)(b) of the Listed Buildings Act 1990. There are five elements which must be present for an object or structure to be listed as a curtilage structure under s.1(5)(b):

---

[71] Inspector's report, para 7.16, 7.17.

[72] Decision 20 August 2007, The Chapel, Sir William Turner's Court, Kirkleatham, Redcar TS10 4QT, Appeal Ref: APP/V0728/E/07/2040520. Listed building consent for its removal was though granted.

[73] Kirkleatham at § 6.

[74] In Northern Ireland the curtilage date under paragraph (b) is "*before 1st October 1973*": Planning Act (Northern Ireland) 2011, s. 80(7).

a. *The object or structure must be within the curtilage of a listed building*

The term "*curtilage*" is not defined in legislation. It covers land which is so intimately associated with a building as to form "*part and parcel*" of that building.[75] In *Methuen-Campbell* Buckley LJ said:[76]

> *"What then is meant by the curtilage of a property? In my judgment it is not sufficient to constitute two pieces of land parts of one and the same curtilage that they should have been conveyed or demised together, for a single conveyance or lease can comprise more than one parcel of land, neither of which need be in any sense an appurtenance of the other or within the curtilage of the other. Nor is it sufficient that they have been occupied together. Nor is the test whether the enjoyment of one is advantageous or convenient or necessary for the full enjoyment of the other. A piece of land may fall clearly within the curtilage of a parcel conveyed without its contributing in any significant way to the convenience or value of the rest of the parcel. On the other hand, it may be very advantageous or convenient to the owner of one parcel of land also to own an adjoining parcel, although it may be clear from the facts that the two parcels are entirely distinct pieces of property. In my judgment, for one corporeal hereditament to fall within the curtilage of another, the former must be so intimately associated with the latter as to lead to the conclusion that the former in truth forms part and parcel of the latter. There can be very few houses indeed that do not have associated with them at least some few square yards of land, constituting a yard or a basement area or passageway or something of the kind, owned and enjoyed with the house, which on a reasonable view could only be regarded as part of the messuage and such small pieces of land would be held to fall within the curtilage of the messuage. This may extend to ancillary buildings, structures or areas such as outhouses, a garage, a driveway, a garden and so forth. How far it is appropriate to regard this identity as parts of one messuage or parcel of*

[75] *Meuthen-Campbell v Walters* [1979] 1 QB 525 at p. 543 as explained and followed by the Court of Appeal in *R (Hampshire County Council) v Blackbushe Airport Ltd* [2021] EWCA Civ 398, [2021] 3 WLR 567.

[76] At 543-544.

> *land as extending must depend on the character and the circumstances of the items under consideration. To the extent that it is reasonable to regard them as constituting one messuage or parcel of land, they will be properly regarded as all falling within one curtilage; they constitute an integral whole."*

The part and parcel test was explained by Andrews LJ in *R (Hampshire County Council) v Blackbushe Airport Ltd ("Hampshire")* :[77]

> *"Of course it does not mean that the yard or garden is literally to be regarded as part of the physical structure of the building. The expression is figurative and means that a reference to that building would be understood to include, or extend to, that other land."*

As an example:[78]

> *"If the building is a dwelling house, then in most cases a reference to the house without more would reasonably be understood to include its yard or garden, or a structure on the adjacent land such as a garage or garden shed. ... it would not be linguistically inaccurate to say that somebody "came round to my house", if in fact they only came to the garden or to a garage at the end of the driveway. Matters would be different, of course, if the garage were located some distance from the house on a different plot of land ..."*

The term has a degree of imprecision; whether land forms part of the curtilage of a building is a question of fact and degree.[79] Planning Practice Guidance 15 (now revoked) provided the following guidance on identifying curtilage:[80]

---

[77] At § 66.

[78] [2021] EWCA Civ 398, [2021] 3 WLR 567 at § 67.

[79] *Skerritts* at §§ 66, 67 per Robert Walker LJ, citing *Dyer v Dorset County Council* [1989] QB 346.

[80] Welsh Office Circular 61/96 contained the same guidance, but is also now cancelled. It has been replaced by Technical Advice Note 24: The Historic Environment. This does not set out guidance on how to identify whether land falls within the curtilage of a building. Current Northern Irish guidance is similar in

"3.34 The principal tests as to whether an object or structure is within the curtilage of a listed building relate to the physical layout of the land surrounding the listed building at the date of the statutory listing and the relationship of the structures on the surrounding land to each other. Changes in ownership, occupation or use after the listing date will not bring about the de-listing of a building which formed part of the principal building at the date of listing. The Courts have held that for a structure or building within the curtilage of a listed building to be part of a listed building it must be ancillary to the principal building, that is it must have served the purposes of the principal building at the date of listing, or at a recent time before the date of listing, in a necessary or reasonably useful way and must not be historically an independent building. Where a self contained building was fenced or walled-off from the remainder of the site at the date of listing, regardless of the purpose for which it was erected and is occupied, it is likely to be regarded as having a separate curtilage. The structure or building must still form part of the land, and this probably means that there must be some degree of physical annexation to the land.

3.35 Considerations which may assist local planning authorities in forming their own views, or giving advice if requested, include:

- the historical independence of the building;

- the physical layout of the principal building and other buildings;

- the ownership of the buildings now and at the time of listing;

- whether the structure forms part of the land;

- the use and function of the buildings, and whether a building is ancillary or subordinate to the principal building."

In the first *Skerritts* case, the Planning Inspector had applied the guidance in PPG 15 on identifying the curtilage and found that "*based on the*

substance to PPG15, see *Criteria for the Scheduling of Historic Monuments and the Listing of Buildings of Special Architectural or Historic Interest, with associated procedures*, para 18.6.

physical, historical, ownership and functional facts" the stable block was curtilage listed. The decision was challenged on the basis that it erred in law of "*overlooking the principle...that the curtilage of a listed building is confined to a small area around the building*". The Court of Appeal applied *Debenhams* and concluded that a curtilage was not confined to a small area around a building. [81] The context of a mansion house, curtilage could cover a significant area and was likely to include stables and outbuildings.

It is important to note, however, that curtilage does not necessarily extend to all land in the same occupation or ownership. Curtilage is a concept relating to a building rather than occupation or ownership of land. In a large estate, the curtilage of the main house may well be less than the land comprised in the estate. For example, in *Dyer v Dorset County Council*,[82] a 100-acre park was not all in the curtilage of the main house. In *McAlpine v Secretary of State for the Environment*,[83] a grassed area used for recreation beyond the formal garden of a large house was held to be outside the curtilage. Nor was the whole of an airport within the curtilage of its terminal building in *Hampshire*.[84] By contrast, in an urban environment, land attached to a dwelling house which is able and intended to be used in conjunction with the house is likely to be within its curtilage.[85]

b. The object or structure must not be fixed to the building otherwise s. 1(5)(a) applies

The question of whether or not an object or structure is fixed to a building is considered in detail above.

---

81 [1987] AC 396.

82 [1989] QB 346.

83 [1995] 1 PLR 16.

84 *Hampshire County Council v Blackbushe Airport Ltd* [2021] EWCA Civ 398, [2021] 3 WLR 567

85 *R (Sumption) v London Borough of Greenwich* [2007] EWHC 2776 (Admin), [2008] 1 P & CR 336.

c. *The object or structure must form part of the land*

Whether an object or structure is part of the land is determined by application of private law principles. These principles, and their application to heritage assets, are considered below.

d. *The object or structure must have been part of the land since before 1 July 1948 in England and Wales or before 1 October 1973 in Northern Ireland*

Determining whether the object was part of the land on 1 July 1948 is a question of fact. A legal issue may arise if the object was part of the land within the curtilage of a listed building before 1948, but was moved to a different part of the land prior to listing.

e. *The object or structure must be ancillary to the listed building*

The concept of a structure having to be ancillary to the main building as well as within its curtilage was raised by Lord Keith in *Debenhams*[86]. He approached the interpretation of what is now s. 1(5) of the Listed Buildings Act 1990 as requiring a principal and accessory relationship. Applying this principle, a building which is not ancillary will not be part of the listed building. It will be separate and may have its own curtilage. A rare case where a building was found to be within a listed curtilage but not ancillary was at Colekitchen Farmhouse, Guildford.[87] A pillbox had been constructed 3.5 metres away from a farmhouse in the Second World War. The Planning Inspector found that the pillbox was not constructed for purposes ancillary to the farmhouse and had not been sued for any ancillary purposes since. He found that it was therefore not listed as a curtilage structure.

[86] [1987] AC 396.

[87] [2009] JPL 1238.

The need for listed building consent

Many of the issues concerning heritage assets and listed building control revolve around the questions considered above: whether the items are lawfully listed buildings or part of listed buildings. It may sometimes be a question whether the act of removing a heritage asset which is listed as a building, or part of a listed building, amounts to works to a listed building for which listed building consent is required.

Section 7 of the Listed Buildings Act 1990 provides that consent is required for (a) "*works for the demolition of a listed building*" or (b) "*works…for its alteration or extension in any manner which would affect its special character as a building of special architectural or historic interest*".

Works for a buildings alteration or extension will only require listed building consent if they would affect the building's special architectural or historic interest whereas all demolition works require consent. This is because demolition works "*would be bound to affect its character as a building of special architectural or historic interest, because if it were not of that character it would not be in the list*" whereas works or alteration or extension may or may not have that effect, hence the qualification which applies for the purposes of s.7.[88]

Where the statue or memorial is caught only by the extended definition then there might be no effect on special interest caused by alteration, for example, because it is a memorial to a person who happened to live in the house but whom is not otherwise historically noteworthy or the artwork is unrelated to the listed building's design. Guidance on special interest is given in the Department of Culture Media and Sports' *Principles of Selection for Listed Buildings* and various selection guides produced by Historic England. These are considered in Chapter 4 below for the light they cast on applications for consent.

Section 8(1) of the Listed Buildings Act 1990 provides that works for alteration or extension are authorised if written consent (referred to as listed building consent) for their execution has been granted by the local

[88] *Shimizu Ltd v Westminster City Council* [1997] 1 WLR 168 at p.181A-B per Lord Hope.

planning authority or the Secretary of State. Section 8(2) provides that for works for the demolition of a listed building, notice of must also be given to the Royal Commission.

Alteration or demolition

Questions can arise as to whether works to a listed building amount to demolition or alteration. This issue arose in *Shimizu Ltd v Westminster City Council*[89] ("*Shimizu*"). Lord Hope, with whom Lords Browne-Wilkinson and Lloyd agreed, stated that "*according to its ordinary meaning, the word "demolish" when used in reference to a building means to pull the building down—in other words, to destroy it completely and break it up*".[90] In *Shimizu* the Court of Appeal had held that the proposed removal of chimney-breasts amounted to works of demolition and not alteration. In doing so, said Lord Hope, the Court of Appeal had fallen into error by applying the words "*demolition*" to a part only of the listed building that is, to the chimney-breasts, not to the whole building.[91] On the distinction between demolition and alteration, he stated:[92]

> *"As I have said, section 8(2) can be read with perfect sense if the word "building" is taken, in the context of these provisions, to mean simply the building or part of a building which is for the time being included in the list as a listed building. If that building or part of a building—the "listed building"—is to be pulled down, so that it will be destroyed completely and broken up, the works will amount to its destruction to which the additional procedure in section 8(2) will always apply. Works which involve the pulling down and breaking up of part of the building, falling short of its destruction, will fall within the expression "alteration" which, if they would affect its character as a building of special architectural or historic interest, will require consent to be sought under section 8(1)."*

89 [1997] 1 WLR 168.

90 *Shimizu* at p.183G.

91 *Shimizu* at p.183 G-H.

92 *Shimizu* at p.185 D-E.

Lord Hope went on to state, however, that the word demolition did not apply only where the proposal was that every single part of a listed building should be pulled down. He stated that removal of so much of an old building as to clear a site for its redevelopment could amount to demolition. Ultimately, in any given case it was a question of fact as to whether the proposed works constitute demolition of the building. Lord Hope went to conclude that earlier works that had been carried out to the listed building – whereby most of the building had been pulled down with the façade and chimney-breasts and chimney-stacks retained – did amount to demolition. He stated:[93]

> *"It is now commonplace, especially in towns and cities, where the exterior of a building contributes to the architectural or historic interest of a group of buildings such as buildings in a terrace, for the facade to be left standing while clearing the remainder of the site for redevelopment. That indeed is what was done in this case. As section 17(3) has envisaged in the case of demolition works, planning permission for the redevelopment of the site was granted at the same time as the original proposals received listed building consent and conservation area consent. It seems to me to be plain that the original proposal was for the demolition of the listed building for all practical purposes, so that a scheme of redevelopment could be carried out. It went far beyond what could reasonably be described as its alteration, as the works were so extensive and so much was to be pulled down and taken away, although the facade and the chimney-breasts and chimney-stacks were to be retained. The question is ultimately one of fact for the decision of the Lands Tribunal, and I do not think that any more precise definition of this expression is required."*

Provided that works are carried out, detaching a fixed statue or memorial from a building is likely to be an alteration. Demolition does not require the entirety of the listed building to be removed, but a clearing of the whole site for practical purposes would suffice.[94] If a statue and its plinth have been listed as a single item, then whether the removal of the statue

---

[93] *Shimizu* at p.185F.

[94] See *Shimizu*; *Walter Lilly & Co Ltd v Clin* [2021] EWCA Civ 136, [2021] 1 WLR 2753.

alone will be demolition will depend on the size of the plinth, and possibly the relative special interest of the elements.[95]

Works at all

Questions can also arise about whether something amounts to "works" at all.[96] For example, if the statue is fixed to plinth or the ground, does work or damage required to remove it constitute demolition? Simply lifting a vase and putting it elsewhere in the garden is hard to characterise as "*works*" or "*demolition*", and a similar view can be taken of lifting a painting off its hook. In practice this often arises first as an aspect of the question whether the item is a listed building or part of it. If an item's removal does not involve works, then it is unlikely to be listed in its own right or on the basis that it is fixed to the building.[97]

Affecting special interest

Listed building consent is only required for works of alteration or extension, as distinct from demolition, if they would affect the special interest of the listed building. That is inevitably a judgement specific to the individual building and proposed works. The list entry provides a starting point for considering special interest, but it is only the more recent entries which either say why the building is of special interest or identify elements which are or are not of such interest. The omission of internal murals from the list entry will usually say nothing about their interest.

There is a useful range of government guidance. Criteria for the identification of listed buildings[98] and assessing significance assist. It is

---

[95] The removal of a curtilage listed building will not be the demolition of the listed building since the principal listed building will remain.

[96] 'Works' involves some degree of physical action, beyond the trivial, for example, painting or repainting: *Royal Borough of Windsor and Maidenhead Council v Secretary of State for the Environment* (1988) 56 P&CR 427 at 431 per Mann J.

[97] See similarly Lord Carnwath's observation that demolition envisages dismantling in *Dill* at §53.

[98] Such as *Principles of Selection for Listing Buildings* (DCMS, November 2018) and Historic England's Selection Guides.

important to have in mind that an effect on special interest, requiring listed building consent to be obtained, is not necessarily harmful. The statutory test is a trigger for a consent to be required. The ultimate conclusion may be that the impact is neutral or positive, but there is still a need to have listed building consent.

Where works of art are considered to be part of the listed building, including by being objects fixed to a building or curtilage listed objects, their removal is likely to affect its special interest if their presence relates to why the building is of special interest. The removal of an item installed as part of the original construction of the building or a remodelling, which has become part of the building, would probably affect special interest. Where the item has been created or arrived more recently there may be more debate whether it contributes to special interest. However historic or architectural interest can change and encompass recent alterations. An example was the Lucian Freud painting *The Study Of Cyclamen* on the plasterwork of his then home, Coombe Priory, in 1956. The early Seventeenth Century house was subsequently listed, without regard to the painting. A later owner removed the mural, with its underlying plaster, when selling the house. The plasterwork/painting was part of the building and the issue was whether its removal had affected the special interest of the listed building. The painting was subsequently returned to the house following an intervention by the local planning authority, but without proceedings being commenced.[99]

Covering up statues and plaques

On some occasions statues, plaques or works of art may be covered up, usually on a temporary basis. This has sometimes been put forward as a short-term solution for contested heritage. Such covers may amount to works requiring listed building consent. The coverings will be works if they are fixed to the listed building (even if not to the statue). A new structure which is extremely close to a listed building but not touching it

[99] Salisbury Journal *Freud mural returned to its Donhead home* 7 December 2012, Daily Mail, *Freud mural returned home safely after being cheekily removed by vendors* 16 January 2013.

might also be works to the building.[100] If works have taken place the question is whether the temporary covering has affected the special interest of the listed building. This will tend to depend on two factors. The first is the significance of the item to the special interest of the listed building. A statue might be an important feature; conversely it may be a very recent addition or be an anomalous plaque. The second factor is whether covering the item harms the appearance or the ability to appreciate other parts of the listed building.

Obtaining a determination whether listed building consent is required

There are a number of mechanisms for establishing whether listed building consent is required.

Certificates of lawfulness of proposed works to listed buildings in England

A certificate of lawfulness of proposed works to listed buildings can be sought from the local planning authority in England.[101] The application is "to *ascertain whether proposed works for the alteration or extension of a listed building in England would be lawful*". If granted, a certificate is conclusive for the next ten years.

The scope of the certificate process is though quite constrained. An application may only relate to an alteration rather than also demolition. For the purposes of a certificate "*works would be lawful if they would not affect the character of the listed building as a building of special architectural or historic interest*".[102] This definition is exhaustive so it is not possible to certify that works would be lawful for other reasons, for example, because they benefit from an extant listed building consent.[103] However, it may

---

[100] *Ampliflaire Ltd v Secretary of State for Scotland* 1999 SLT 937.

[101] Listed Buildings Act 1990, s. 26H(1).

[102] Listed Buildings Act 1990, s. 26H(2).

[103] *R(France) v Royal Borough of Kensington and Chelsea* [2017] EWCA Civ 429, [2017] 1 WLR 3206 at §72 per Hickinbottom LJ. The Court held that it was not possible to certify that works would be lawful because a listed building consent for

be possible to secure a certificate on the basis that the works will not affect special interest because the item being altered/removed is not part of the building or within the extended definition.

A decision that no action should be taken on a listed building consent application

On considering a listed building consent application the local planning authority or a Minister or Inspector on appeal may decide that consent is not required.[104] It would then take no action and that would be a sufficient determination. This approach was taken in *Chambers v Guildford Borough Council* ("*Chambers*").[105]

Resisting enforcement proceedings

Where works have been carried out, the local planning authority[106] may issue a listed building enforcement notice, requiring the undoing of the harm or remedial action. It is a ground of appeal that listed building consent was not required.[107] That ground includes all potential bases for the works being lawful, including that correctly interpreted the list does not include the building, the object or structure is not within the extended definition of fixed or curtilage items, or that the building on the list is not a building.[108] Separately it is also a ground of appeal in England and Wales that the building is not of special interest and should be delisted.[109]

In criminal proceedings for carrying out works without listed building consent the prosecution must prove that the works were to a listed

---

them had been implemented, although upholding the council's conclusion that the works would be lawful.

[104] *Chambers v Guildford Borough Council* [2008] EWHC 826 (QB).

[105] [2008] EWHC 826 (QB).

[106] Or, much more rarely, the Minister or the Department.

[107] Listed Buildings Act 1990, s. 39((1)(c); Planning Act (Northern Ireland) 2011, s. 159(1)(b).

[108] *Dill* at § 25 per Lord Carnwath JSC.

[109] Listed Buildings Act 1990, s.39((1)(a).

building.[110] So it is possible to contend that the item was not a building or was outwith the extended definition. Again, the issue may arise if an injunction is sought[111] to enforce against an alleged breach of listed building control.

It is, of course, far better to identify and resolve issues as to whether listed building consent before works are carried out and potential criminal liability incurred.

Declaratory proceedings in the High Court

The High Court is able to pronounce on legal rights in the event of a dispute. Applications for declarations on the status of land have been sought throughout the history of the planning regime. However these often raise matters of fact, benefitting from a site visit, and matters of judgement. The more recent preference of the Courts has been to discourage such proceedings when there are alternative planning mechanisms available.[112] In *Chambers* the High Court stayed an application for a declaration that a pillbox in the grounds of a farmhouse was not curtilage listed. The Court considered that it was better to resolve the issue by the local authority or Minister deciding whether to proceed with an application for listed building consent.

Alteration of the list

It is possible for the list entry to be altered to specifically exclude the item, whether on the basis that it is not part of the building or within the extended definition, or because it is not of special interest. This power is available in all jurisdictions since a listing may be of only part of a building.[113] The extended definition can be excluded by clear enough language since "*It is clear that a part only of a single building, if such it be*

[110] *Dill* at § 24 per Lord Carnwath JSC.

[111] Under Listed Buildings Act 1990, s 44A; Planning Act (Northern Ireland) 2011, s. 156.

[112] *R (on the application of Reprotech (Pebsham) Ltd) v East Sussex County Council* [2002] UKHL 8, [2003] 1 WLR 348

[113] *Shimizu (UK) Ltd v Westminster City Council* [1997] 1 WLR 168.

can be, listed without that having the effect that the whole of the building becomes listed under section 1(5), because it would otherwise be pointless to have the power to list only part of a building".[114]

It is also possible for an entry to identify parts of the listed building which are not of special interest.

In England s. 1(5A) of the Listed Buildings Act says that any list entry:[115]

> "*... may provide—*
>
> *(a) that an object or structure mentioned in subsection (5)(a) or (b) is not to be treated as part of the building for the purposes of this Act;*
>
> *(b) that any part or feature of the building is not of special architectural or historic interest.*"

There is little in the way of statutory procedures for altering the list. If the Secretary of State proposes to amend the list in England then consultation must take place with Historic England and with "*such other persons or bodies of persons as appear to [the Minister] appropriate as having special knowledge of, or interest in, buildings of architectural or historic interest*".[116] The Welsh Ministers must serve notice on the owner and occupier of the building, the local planning authority and those with specialist knowledge or interest whom they consider appropriate to consult before adding or removing a building from the list.[117] This Welsh duty does not extend to other amendments to the list. In Northern

---

[114] *R (Hammerton) v London Underground Limited* [2002] EWHC 2307 (Admin) at § 168 per Ouseley J. The Minister had listed the Braithwaite Viaduct which was part of the Bishopsgate Goods Yard complex on the edge of the City of London. Her expressed decision not to list any more of the Goods Yard was not bypassed by the extended definition in s. 1(5) of the Listed Buildings Act 1990.

[115] Inserted by the Enterprise and Regulatory Reform Act 2013, Sch.17 §8 with effect from 25 June 2013.

[116] Listed Buildings Act, s. 1(4).

[117] Listed Buildings Act, s. 2A.

Ireland the Department must consult with the appropriate council and the Historic Buildings Council before compiling or amending any list.[118]

None of the provisions specifies a procedure for applying for a change in the list or de-listing of the building, but since there is power to change the list a request can be entertained. In England the process is administered by Historic England. A request can be made either using their free service or on a paid for basis under their Enhanced Advisory Service for Fast-Track Listing or Listing Enhancement.[119] Under those arrangements Historic England will make their recommendation to the Minister within a guaranteed timeframe, usually 12 weeks. However starting any delisting or amendment process is discretionary and:[120]

> *"Applications for de-listing will not generally be considered if: the building has had a repairs notice served on it; or is currently the subject of an appeal against refusal of consent; or if a prosecution or enforcement action of any kind, is in hand. Both listed building consent appeal and enforcement appeal procedures give appellants the right to argue that a building is not of special interest and should be removed from the List. Where one of these processes is already underway, the issue of de-listing is more properly addressed as part of that process.*
>
> *[Historic England] would be unlikely to carry out an assessment for de-listing if works are imminent, underway, or listed building consent has been applied for or granted, unless a decision on de-listing would be helpful to inform the listed building consent process. The decision on whether to take an assessment forward in these circumstances is made on a case-by-case basis in consultation with the owner and the local planning authority as appropriate."*

Requests to alter the list in Wales should be made to Cadw, and in Northern Ireland to the Historic Environment Division, Historic

---

[118] Planning Act (Northern Ireland) 2011, s. 80(3).

[119] Further details are provided in *Removing a Building from the List* (Historic England, January 2019).

[120] *Removing a Building from the List.*

Buildings Designation Branch of the Department for Communities. In Northern Ireland, guidance is given in De-listing: Removing a building from the list of buildings of special architectural or historic interest.[121]

An application for an amendment of the list entry or delisting would require supporting evidence which may include an expert view of a heritage consultant on special interest or legal advice.

Informal views

In practice it may be possible to obtain a view from the local planning authority's conservation officer whether a particular item is part of a listed building and whether listed building consent is required for its removal. Strictly that will not be binding on the local authority, any other person or the courts, but it would be difficult for the authority to change its mind and bring proceedings. A change of position by the authority would need careful justification.

Written reassurance would usually be sufficient for the status of the item to be accepted by other authorities, such as HMRC or the Arts Council England in an export licensing application.

Any such opinion of the authority should be set out in writing. It is important that the judgement is adequately informed, so the owner needs to have explained the circumstances in writing, setting out the relevant facts. It may be useful for that explanation to be accompanied by a legal opinion.

Cadw or Historic England might also be involved in any consideration. That is particularly likely if a grade I or II* listed building is involved.

[121] Department for Communities, February 2021.

Status of listed building or object forming part of listed building once removed

Questions can arise as to the status of a listed building, or object forming part of a listed building, once it is removed.

Removal without consent

The position where all or part of a listed building has been removed without consent has been considered in a number of cases.

R v Leominster District Council ex p Antique Country Buildings Ltd[122] concerned a timber frame barn at Stagbatch Farm, near Leominster, which had been erected prior to 1620 and which was listed grade II. The barn had been dismantled in 1985 and the 70-80% of the timber framing sold with the intention that it be exported by the United States of America. Only the foundations and footings remained on the site of the barn.

The local planning authority subsequently obtained an injunction preventing the removal of the timbers from England and Wales and ultimately took custody of them. It then issued two listed building enforcement notices, with the various parties, including those who had bought the timbers after the building had been dismantled, being served with a copy notice as 'owner' of the building. The purchasers challenged the notices on the basis that they were not owners of the building or part of it and that restoration was not possible.

In the injunction proceedings Hoffmann J held that the timbers could still be described as a building, on the basis that in the context of a listed building enforcement notice "*the word "building" is perfectly capable of meaning something which had been a listed building but which had since been demolished.*" In the subsequent judicial review Mann J said:

> *"I turn to the question of whether the applicants, being the owners of the disassembled parts, are capable of being the owners of a listed building. Mr. Hockman says that pieces are personalty and are not a*

[122] (1987) 56 P&CR 240.

building as described in section 290(1) of the Act albeit they could be and were to be re-erected. I am not persuaded by this argument. The translation from realty to personalty with the prospect of reincarnation as a corporeal hereditament does not seem to me to be relevant. He who owns the parts owns the building. Any other conclusion would allow an evaporation of the built environment dependent on whether or not the owner of the site disposed of the re-erectable remnants. The parts must of course be fairly describable as "the building." A single block from the previous London Bridge would not in any ordinary use of language entitle the owner of the block to describe himself as the owner of London Bridge. Ownership of 70–80 per cent, of the components would render him capable of so describing himself. The applicants in this case could properly be regarded as owners and accordingly this ground of challenge fails."

On that analysis, the owner of parts which amount to a substantial part of the building would still be an owner for the purposes of enforcement. The judge's comments about a block from the previous London Bridge are in the context of the impossibility of restoring a building from many thousands of elements scattered amongst individual owners. This suggests that where a building cannot be restored it may cease to be a building for the purposes of the Listed Buildings Act 1990. However a single item of heritage significance removed from a much larger building would still be part of the listed building since its restoration could be required: for example, a statue, a relief or a fireplace, and this is discussed further below.

Mann J also held that if sufficient parts of the building remained so that putting back the building could be described as 'restoration', then a listed building enforcement notice could be issued for that purpose.[123] It should be noted, however, that if restoration was not possible a notice could require works to alleviate the effects of the unlawful works.[124] This could extend to constructing a replica of the whole or part (such replacing a plinth).

---

123 *Leominster* at 247.

124 Listed Buildings Act, s 38(2)(b).

The decision of Sullivan J in *Judge v First Secretary of State* ("*Judge*") is also of assistance, although it did not concern removal of a listed building without consent. [125] *Judge* concerned a challenge to the grant of listed building consent for the relocation of the Sir Samuel Sadler statue in Victoria Square, Middlesbrough. As part of a scheme for an art gallery and the rearrangement of the square, the statue was to be moved to another position in the square. The claimant complained that the consent could not cover relocation. Sullivan J summarised the argument and explained:

> *"17. ... The claimant contends that it was not open to the first defendant to grant consent to "relocate the statue" because once the statue has been moved, it will cease to be part of the land and the various component parts will become chattels, divorced from the land. Whether or not that is so as a matter of property law is, in my judgment, wholly irrelevant. Planning is a statutory code and the claimant correctly submitted that the task of the court is to further Parliament's intention by applying that code.*
>
> *18. If one looks at sections 7 and 17 which I have set out above, it is plain that listed building consent can be given for the demolition of a listed building subject to a condition that the building must be reconstructed, either in whole or in part. That is plainly within the powers conferred by the code, even though it may well be the case that, pending reconstruction, various component parts of a listed building, for example, the timbers from a timber framed house, will have become detached from the land."*

He then quoted Hoffmann and Mann JJ in the *Leominster* judgments and said:[126]

> *"Their judgments are not binding upon me, but I find them wholly persuasive. In the context of listed buildings legislation, it is simply*

---

[125] [2005] EWHC 887 (Admin), [2006] JPL 996.

[126] *Judge* at §20. Permission to appeal was dismissed by the Court of Appeal: [2005] EWCA Civ 1155.

> *irrelevant to consider whether or not there has been a "translation from realty to personalty"."*

In *Dill*[127] Lord Carnwath JSC approved *Judge* in respect of the:

> *"question whether the dismantled components of something which had unquestionably been a listed building could, by the process of dismantling, become chattels rather than "buildings" and thereby lose their statutory protection as such. Not surprisingly the court rejected that interpretation as wholly incompatible with the purpose of the legislation."*

Leominster, Judge and *Dill* support the conclusion that if a listed building is dismantled, or elements are removed from it, then those removed parts are still part of the listed building and listed building control will apply to them if they are removed without consent. In the examples of contested heritage, a statue or plaque which has been removed in breach of a requirement for listed building consent would remain part of the listed building. Enforcement measures, including the issue of a listed building enforcement notice, would be available in respect of them.

The *Leominster, Judge* and *Dill* line of cases do not address the position where the building, or part of it, has been destroyed, in that the parts have been reduced to a condition that they cannot be reintegrated into the building (even with new material) and lack any heritage value. Legally that leads to two possibilities: that they remain part of the listed building but no further control or enforcement applies; or the pieces cease to be listed once they are incapable of being used in the restoration of the building and have lost any heritage value. The latter proposition is not on the face of the statute, but there is support in the comments of Mann J in *Leominster* for the conclusion that the impossibility of restoring a building might lead to the conclusion that it is no longer a building for the purposes of listed building control. In most cases, the issue is unlikely to arise in practice. In circumstances where reconstruction or reinstatement are not possible, there would be no purpose in taking action to preserve the remains. A pile of rubble may be just a pile of

[127] *Dill* at §55.

rubble. However, a fragment which showed, say, an Anglo-Saxon carving or a rare construction technique might still be of historic or architectural interest. In such a case there may still be value in taking action to preserve the item. The question may arise whether on a purposive approach to the legislation, such remains could still be part of the listed building.

To the extent that the caselaw touches upon it, the owner of land from which the listed building was removed will remain an owner for enforcement purposes. In *Leominster* a copy of the listed building enforcement notice was served on Mrs Davenport, the owner of the land where the barn had been situated. She did not contest the appeal but there was no suggestion that she was not properly a target of the notice. Similarly in *Dill*, no appeal was brought at any stage by Mr Dill on the basis that a listed building enforcement notice could not be issued in respect of land, or a copy served on him as owner, when the listed items had been removed entirely and were no longer in his ownership. As one option will be requiring the listed building to be returned to the site, the ability to require the landowner to accept it back (and to tell them to recover it) is supported by a purposive approach to the legislation.

<u>*Removal with listed building consent*</u>

If an item is removed with listed building consent then its future status will depend on the meaning of the consent. For example, if the consent allows the removal of the item without including a condition as to what should be done with it, then the item will no longer be listed once removed (such as a chandelier being sold). A consent which requires the item to be replaced in the same or another location will keep it under listed building control. This is what happened in the *Judge* case, where consent required reconstruction of the statue at another specified location within one year of its removal. It does not follow that all listed building consents will specify what must happen to the listed building following its removal: a consent may simply authorise its removal. [128]

[128] *Dill* at § 45 (quoting Inspector's decision §§ 48 to 52), §§ 97 to 100 per Singh J, discussed further below. This conclusion was undisturbed on appeal.

The status of different elements

A listed statue may consist of several elements. To take a common example: the statue itself, a plinth (which might itself be made from stone blocks cemented together) and a base. Where a listed building has different elements, questions may arise as to the status of different elements where some are removed, some are destroyed and others remain on the original site.

Where part of a listed building is removed and part remains, the part which has been removed will remain part of the listed building for the reasons discussed above. A listed building enforcement notice could be issued to require its restoration in situ, or an injunction obtained for those purposes.

Where the part of the building which has been removed has been broken up in such a way that it cannot be rebuilt or reinstated, the case law (discussed above) suggests that this will cease to be part of the listed building but the position is not free from doubt. As to the remaining part, the position is that unless and until the building was delisted, there would in law be a listed building there. The base would remain part of the listed building. The only issue would then be whether further works to it would require listed building consent. It would be a matter of judgement whether works to the base would affect the special interest of the listed building. It may be that the remaining part has no heritage value, so that further works would not affect its special architectural or historic interest.

Applications for listed building consent

Listed building consent is applied for to the local planning authority[129] (usually the district or unitary council).

The local authority's application form must be used and the application accompanied by 'such plans, drawings and information as are necessary

[129] Listed Buildings Act 1990, s. 10.

to describe the works'.[130]The application must also be accompanied by a design and access statement ("DAS") which will deal with, along with access, "the design principles and concepts that have been applied to the works and how they have been applied to take account of the special architectural or historic importance of the building; the particular physical features of the building that justify its designation as a listed building; and the building's setting.[131] The application must in practice be accompanied by the justification for the proposal. This may be included in the DAS or supplementing it.

The High Court in *Dill* held that the Inspector had been wrong to find that the listed building consent application was invalid because it failed to specify where the items would be removed to: given the application made, such details were not required. Implicitly if consent had been given for the removal of the urns and piers, they would have lost any listed status which they had.

In England the local planning authority is required to consult Historic England and the National Amenity Societies on certain listed building applications.[132] The National Amenity Societies are the Society for the Protection of Ancient Buildings, the Ancient Monuments Society, the Council for British Archaeology, the Georgian Group, the Victorian Society and the Twentieth Century Society. The consultation duties are principally contained in the Arrangements for Handling Heritage Applications – Notification to Historic England and National Amenity Societies and the Secretary of State (England) Direction 2021. These

---

[130] Planning (Listed Buildings and Conservation Areas) Regulations 1990, reg 3(1); Planning (Listed Buildings and Conservation Areas) (Wales) Regulations 2012, reg 3(1). The Planning (Listed Buildings) Regulations (Northern Ireland) 2015, reg 2 is to a similar effect in respect of drawings but does not require the use of an application form. A form is though available and ought to be used.

[131] Planning (Listed Buildings and Conservation Areas) Regulations 1990, reg 3A; Planning (Listed Buildings) Regulations (Northern Ireland) 2015, reg 4; Planning (Listed Buildings and Conservation Areas) (Wales) Regulations 2012, reg 6 (which add appearance, environmental sustainability, layout and scale).

[132] The provisions are summarised in the Planning Practice Guidance, ID: 18a-069-20190723.

replaced a previous direction as part of the Robert Jenrick package of controls on contested heritage cases.

As particularly relevant to artworks and contested heritage items which are listed in their own right, the local planning authority are required to notify Historic England of listed building consent applications for works:[133]

(i) in respect of any grade I or II* listed building;

(ii) relevant works in respect of a grade II listed building. Relevant works include:[134] (a) the demolition of any principal building; and (b) commemorative object works.

A principal building is a building shown on the list and any object or structure fixed to it, but does not include a curtilage listed building.[135] Commemorative object works are "*works for the full or part demolition of a statue, monument, memorial or plaque that are, or are part of, a listed building*".[136]

The National Amenity Societies must be notified of listed building consent applications for works:

(i) for the demolition of a listed building (of any grade); or

(ii) for works for the alteration of a listed building which comprise or include the demolition of any part of that building.

If the local planning authority intend to grant listed building consent then they must first notify the Secretary of State if:[137]

---

133 Notification Direction 2021, para 4(b).

134 Relevant works also include the demolition of a principal external wall or all or a substantial part of the interior of a principal building.

135 Notification Direction, para 3.

136 Notification Direction, para 3.

137 This is the result of a general obligation to refer listed building consent applications to the Secretary of State where there is an intention to grant consent (Listed Buildings

(a) the works are to a grade I or II* listed building or are relevant works to a grade II listed building (including commemorative object works); and

(b) no objection has been received from Historic England or a National Amenity Society pursuant to notice under the Direction.

The authority may not issue the consent within 28 days of giving such notice unless the Minister says otherwise.[138] The Minister may call in the application for her own determination or extend the time for considering whether to do so.[139]

In Greater London a local planning authority may only grant listed building consent for works to a grade I or II* listed building or relevant works to a grade II listed building if the consent or at the direction of Historic England.[140]

If the local planning authority is making the listed building consent application to itself then it must notify Historic England and the National Amenity Societies of the application. If any of those bodies object and the local planning authority does not propose to refuse the application then the authority must make an application to the Secretary of State for consent.[141] Local planning authorities in Wales do not have to notify the Welsh Ministers if they intend to approve applications which affect only the interior of grade II listed buildings.[142] Additionally the Welsh Ministers have agreed that some Welsh authorities need not refer other applications on grade II buildings (other than demolition) if they intend to approve in accordance with specialist heritage advice or

Act, s 13) and the exclusion of most such applications by Notification Direction 2021, para 5.

[138] Listed Buildings Act 1990, s. 13(3).

[139] Listed Buildings Act 1990, ss. 12 and 13(2)(b) respectively.

[140] Listed Buildings Act 1990, s. 14. The general obligation to obtain Historic England's approval is cut down by Notification Direction 2021, § 6.

[141] Planning (Listed Buildings and Conservation Areas) Regulations 1990, reg 13.

[142] Direction referred to in TAN24, § 5.20.

the agreement of Cadw.[143] Councils in Northern Ireland must refer all applications for listed building consent which they intend to approve to the Department for Infrastructure for possible call-in unless the approval would be in accordance with the advice from the Department for Communities.[144]

Conclusions on the need for listed building consent in relation to heritage assets

In summary, the following analysis would apply to works affecting the following types of heritage assets.

Assets which are part of larger structures, such as statues fixed outside buildings, or plaques

For assets which are fixed to a building, two questions arise. The first is whether or not the building is listed. Whether or not it is listed can be determined by searching the relevant electronic database. If the building is listed, the question is then whether the asset is "fixed" to the building. Whether a structure or object is fixed or is part of the land under the extended definition in s.1(5)(a) is judged by application of the two-stage test derived from property law: (1) the method and degree of annexation and (2) the purpose of annexation.

Freestanding statues

Freestanding statues will only be covered by the listed building regime if they are listed as a building in their own right. Whether or not it is listed can be determined by searching the relevant electronic database.

If the statue is listed in its own right, consideration should be given to whether it is capable of being a building for the purposes of s.1(5) of the Listed Buildings Act 1990. In accordance with the Supreme Court

---

[143] See TAN24, para 5.21 and *Invitation to Apply for Listed Building Consent Delegation.*

[144] Planning Act (Northern Ireland) 2011, ss. 88, 89 and Listed Buildings (Removal of Duty to Notify) (Northern Ireland) Direction 2017.

decision in *Dill* that question should be answered by approached in the same way as it is in planning law – applying the test from *Skerritts,* i.e. by considering its size, permanence and degree of physical attachment

If the statue is capable of being a building for the purposes of s. 1(5), then consideration should be given to whether the proposed work requires listed building consent.

Statues on plinths or other bases

For statutes on plinths or other bases, consideration needs to be given to whether the statue is listed alone, or together with the plinth or base, in its own right, or whether the plinth or base is listed and the statue is part of that larger structure.

The more likely scenario is that the statue is listed together with the plinth or base. As with freestanding statutes, consideration needs to be given to whether it is capable of being a building for the purposes of s.1(5) of the Listed Buildings Act 1990. If the statue is affixed to a plinth or base, which in turn is affixed to the ground, that is a factor that would support the conclusion that the item is capable of being a building for the purpose of s.1(5).

CHAPTER TWO

PLANNING PERMISSION

When considering the removal or alteration of a heritage asset, it is necessary to determine whether planning permission is required.

Works which affect land and the use of land are controlled by the planning system by requiring planning permission for the carrying out of development.[145] Section 55(1) of the Town and Country Planning Act ("TCPA"), defines "development" as, subject to various exceptions, the carrying out of building, engineering, mining or other operations in, on, over or under land or the making of any material change in the use of any buildings or land.[146] In summary, a planning application would need to be made and approved for:

a. The removal or demolition of a heritage asset comprising a building which is 50 m^3 or more in volume[147] or, in England, comprises a statue, monument or memorial and is a building in its own right.

b. The removal or alteration of a heritage asset from a building where the removal or alteration amounts to building operations: (i) materially affects the external appearance of the building; and, (ii) does not benefit from permitted development rights.

c. Any alteration or demolition which is contrary to a condition on a planning permission which is in effect on the site where the heritage asset is located.

---

[145] Town and Country Planning Act 1990, s 57; Planning Act (Northern Ireland) 2011, s. 24(1).

[146] For the similar legislation in Northern Ireland see Planning Act (Northern Ireland) 2011, s. 23(1).

[147] The minimum volume is 115 m^3 in Northern Ireland.

Demolition in a conservation area is subject to additional rules on relevant demolition or conservation area consent. This is addressed in Chapter 3 below.

Heritage assets which are not fixed to the outside of a building, or which are not buildings in their own right, are not subject to planning control, unless subject to planning conditions attaching to a particular planning permission.

The installation of an artwork might amount to operational development requiring planning permission (but not if inside an existing building). In some circumstances changing to use land for display of artworks could be a material change of use,[148] but individual items will usually not alter the use or be ancillary (and so within) the primary use.

There are four questions to consider when determining whether removal or alteration of a heritage asset requires planning permission on account of it being a building in its own right or part of a building:

a. Whilst not determinative, is the asset a building or part of a building for the purposes of the TCPA?

b. Are the proposed works development within the meaning of the TCPA?

c. Are there relevant permitted development rights?

[148] The use of land as a museum or art gallery are recognised uses in planning terms. A use including the "*display of art installations*" at Brunswick and Columbia Wharf, Hackney, was found a material change of use: Planning Inspector's appeal decision, ref APP/U3560/C/19/3242430 (10 January 2022). In earlier interim injunction proceedings in that case, the High Court found that floating five sharks constructed of fibre glass and polystyrene, containing smoke machines, lasers and loudspeakers, on a raft in the Regent's Canal was arguably a material change of use: *London Borough of Hackney v Shiva Limited* [2020] EWHC 2489 (QB). That the sharks would sing Charles Trenet's *La Mer*, in French, and give important themes in contemporary architecture and urbanism, was not sufficient to prevent the injunction being granted.

d. Is there a relevant condition attached to an existing planning permission?

Building or part of a building

A useful and often decisive preliminary question in determining whether planning permission is required to remove or alter a heritage asset is whether the asset is a building or part of a building for the purposes of the TCPA. If what was created was a building, then its removal is likely to be a building operation requiring planning permission. A building is defined in the TCPA as including "*any structure or erection and any part of a building*" but "*does not include plant or machinery comprised in a building*".[149]

As discussed in Chapter 2 in the context of the listed building regime, the test for determining whether something is a building for the purposes of the TCPA is that derived from the judgment of Schiemann LJ in the Court of Appeal in *Skerritts of Nottingham v Secretary of State for the Environment, Transport and the Regions (No.2) ("Skerritts")*: whether something is a building is to be judged by considering its size, permanence and degree of physical attachment.[150] The application of the test requires an evaluative judgement to be made; where the relevant decision-maker directs him or herself by reference to the *Skerritts* test and arrives at a rationally defensible conclusion, the decision on the application of the statutory definition will be upheld as lawful.[151]

---

[149] Town and Country Planning Act 1990, s. 336(1); Planning Act (Northern Ireland) 2011, s. 250(1).

[150] [2000] JPL 1025 at 1031. As Lord Carnwath JSC noted in his judgment in *Dill v Secretary of State for Communities and Local Government* [2020] UKSC 20, [2020] 1 WLR 2206 (at §46), the formulation can be traced back through the leading planning case on the definition of "building" in the planning statutes (*Barvis Ltd v Secretary of State for the Environment* (1971) 22 P & CR 710, DC) to the judgment of Jenkins J in the rating case of *Cardiff Rating Authority v Guest Keen Baldwin's Iron and Steel Co Ltd* [1949] 1 KB 385.

[151] *Dill* at §46 per Lord Carnwath.

There is limited assistance in the cases as to how the buildings test will be applied in practice to heritage assets. The planning court cases have tended to involve large structures. However, what these cases show is that the term "building" in the TCPA has a wide definition and has been interpreted by the courts to include structures which would not ordinarily be described as buildings.

a. *Skerritts* concerned a marquee erected annually in the grounds of a hotel and retained on site between February and October. It was 40m long, some 17m wide and 5m tall. Its erection took a number of days and multiple erectors. It was held in place by its own considerable weight, internal bracing and ground spikes. The inspector concluded that "*as a matter of fact and degree, the marquee, due to its ample dimensions, its permanent rather than fleeting character and the secure nature of its anchorage, is a structure which is to be regarded as a building for planning purposes*".[152] The inspector's reasoning was upheld by the Court of Appeal.

b. *Barvis* related to the erection of a moveable tower crane, approximately 89 feet high. Bridge J concluded that the "*enormous crane*" was a "*building*". This conclusion was not displaced by the fact that it had a limited degree of mobility, having been placed on rails on the site, nor by the fact that it would, in the future, be dismantled and re-erected at another site:[153]

c. *Hall Hunter Partnership v First Secretary of State*[154] concerned the erection of 39 hectares of polytunnels. The inspector had concluded that the polytunnels were buildings having regard to their size, degree or physical attachment and permanence, a decision that Sullivan J upheld on appeal to the High Court under s.289 of the TCPA. As to size, the Inspector concluded concluded that "*the polytunnels to which the notice was directed*

[152] See *Dill* at §51.

[153] *Barvis Ltd v Secretary of State for the Environment* (1971) 22 P & CR 710, DC, at pp. 715-716 per Bridge J.

[154] [2006] EWHC 3482 (Admin), [2007] JPL 1023.

were, as a matter of fact and degree, of substantial size and proportion". The inspector concluded that the polytunnels had a substantial degree of physical attachment to the ground, in view of the fact that machines were used to screw the vast number of legs up to one metre into the ground. As to permanence, this did not connote a state of affairs which was to continue forever or indefinitely. The fact that a large and well-constructed structure was capable of being dismantled and removed annually was not determinative. It was enough that the polytunnels remained in one particular location for three months.

d. *R (on the application of Save Woolley Valley) v Bath and North East Somerset Council*[155] concerned mobile poultry units being 20m x 6m x 3.5 metres in height, weighing 2 tonnes and housing 1,000 laying hens. The units were not generally fixed to the ground but were mounted on metal skids to allow them to slide along the ground. The Council had concluded, applying the *Skerritts* test, that although the "sheer size, weight and bulk" of the units pointed towards a finding that they were "buildings". However, these factors were outweighed by the fact that the units were not attached to the ground, and were mobile. The Council's decision was overturned by the High Court on judicial review, with Lang J concluded that the Council had taken too narrow approach to the meaning of building. Lang J noted that the term building had been given a wide meaning, including structures which would ordinarily be described as buildings. The ability to move them around the field did not remove the significance of their presence in planning terms: the units were permanently in their field, and there was no limit on the length of time they would remain there – they could be there for years. The Council were required to reconsider whether they were buildings.

A rare Planning Inspector's decision on whether the erection of a sculpture required planning permission is 34-35 Cadogan Place, London SW1.[156] The owner of a maisonette proposed to erect a stainless steel

[155] [2012] EWHC 2161 (Admin), [2013] Env LR 8.

[156] Appeal Ref: APP/K5600/X/10/2140909 (2nd March 2011).

sculpture, mounted on a metal frame, within their courtyard. The proposal was to replace an almost identical work already in place in the courtyard. The replacement sculpture would be 5.5m tall, 6.4m wide, with the metal frame's 'legs' set into a raised planting bed and sliding spring bolts holding it to adjoining walls (replacing the permanent attachments of the existing sculpture). An appeal for a certificate that planning permission was not required was dismissed. The Inspector applied the size, permanence and physical attachment tests. He noted that the existing sculpture was delivered in separate pieces and welded or bolted together and attached to the frame, a process that took three days. The inspector concluded that the installation was akin to operations normally undertaken by a builder and so was a building operation requiring planning permission.

A post-*Dill* planning enforcement appeal which applied the size, permanence and physical attachment factors concerned land at Brunswick and Columbia Wharf, Hackney. The Inspector found that the erection of three "art installations", in the form of shelters of varying artistic attributes sited on the roof of a building were building operations. The items were constructed on site from multiple parts, substantial in size and had varying degrees of fixing.[157] Two other installations, an inflatable performance space on a floating barge and five full-scale fibreglass sharks intended to float in a breaching position in the canal, were treated as part of a mixed use of the land which included art installations. The Inspector suggested that "*externally displayed art installations generally require planning permission in their own right and that those that may not will in my view be unlikely to be harmful*".[158] That is perhaps too much of a generalisation. The size, permanence and attachment are fact sensitive and it may be difficult to characterise placing a single piece item as a building operation.

In summary, the following approach to the question of whether a heritage asset is a building finds support in the case law.

---

[157] At § 24 to 26.

[158] At § 168.

First, a large heritage asset, placed in a public location, is likely to be a building, either taken together with a plinth, or freestanding as it will be fair sized, is likely to be fixed in place, provided though that it is on permanent display.

Secondly, an asset being on short term display or loan will be relevant to whether it is a building for the purposes of the TCPA. Whilst "permanence" is a relevant factor when determining whether an item is a building, the planning court cases discussed above emphasise that permanence has to be construed in terms of significance in the planning context. In *Skerritts* Schiemann L.J. said of permanence: "*in situ for how long, to which I would answer: for a sufficient length of time to be of significance in the planning context*".[159] "*It is matter of degree between the temporary and the everlasting*" (see).[160] In *Hall Hunter* for the very large polytunnels to remain in one particular location for three months was found by the inspector to be sufficient to be of consequence in the planning context. Applying this reasoning, the fact that a heritage asset, for example a statue, has been installed for a limited period of time would not preclude it from constituting a building for the purposes of the TCPA.

For heritage assets which are, potentially, part of a building, the question whether they are part of that building appears to be judged on the purpose and degree of annexation. This is the test applied to whether an object is fixed to a listed building and would appear to be of general application to whether in planning terms something is part of a building: see *Corthorn Land and Timber Co Ltd v Minister of Housing and Local Government*[161], discussed in *Dill.* When looking at the purpose of annexation, there is broad distinction to be made between the display of a work of art for its own appreciation and its display as part of the design of the building. Only the latter example would be fixed to the building. Works which are permanently fixed to the exterior of a building would likely be part of the building, given the strength of the annexation. This is likely to be the case even if it could be said that the purpose of their

[159] *Skerritts* at p. 1034.

[160] *Skerritts* at p. 1036 per Morritt LJ.

[161] (1965) 17 P & CR 210.

fixation is to enable the appreciation of the work, since there will also be an effect on the design of the building.

If a heritage asset is not a building or part of a building then its removal is not likely to be seen as a building, engineering or other operation and so capable of being development.[162] In such cases planning permission for its removal will not be required.

Is the proposed activity development?

If a heritage asset is a building or part of a building the next question which arises is whether the proposed works are building operations for the purposes of the TCPA. Development is defined as the carrying out of "*building, engineering, mining or other operations in, on, over or under land, or the making of any material change in the use of any buildings or other land*".[163] Building operations include the demolition of a building (subject to important exceptions discussed below), "*structural alterations of or additions to buildings*" and other operations normally undertaken by a builder.[164]

The following operations are expressly excluded from the statutory definition of development[165]: the carrying out for the maintenance, improvement or other alteration of any building of works which (i) affect only the interior of the building, or (ii) do not materially affect the

[162] Under Town and Country Planning Act 1990, s. 55(1); Planning Act (Northern Ireland) 2011, s. 23(1).

[163] Town and Country Planning Act 1990, ss. 55(1); Planning Act (Northern Ireland) 2011, ss. 23(1), 24(1). In art cases, material changes of use are predominantly only relevant in changes to an art gallery or something similar, rather than controlling removal.

[164] Town and Country Planning Act 1990, s. 55(1A); Planning Act (Northern Ireland) 2011, s. 23(2).

[165] Town and Country Planning Act 1990, s. 55(2)(a); Planning Act (Northern Ireland) 2011, s. 23(3)(a).

external appearance of the building. This exception applies only to an existing building.[166]

In addition, the TCPA provides that the Secretary of State may issue a direction providing that the certain descriptions of demolition are excluded from the definition of development for the purposes of the TCPA.[167] Previously, in England, minor categories of demolition were excluded from the definition of development (and so do not need planning permission) by the Town and Country Planning (Demolition – Description of Buildings) Direction 2014. These included the demolition of the whole of "*any building the cubic content of which, measured externally, does not exceed 50 cubic metres*".[168] As most individual statues and memorials are less than 50 m³ in volume[169], the 2014 Direction had the effect that planning permission was not required for the complete demolition of smaller heritage assets. However, on 21 April 2021, the Town and Country Planning (Demolition – Description of Buildings) Direction 2021[170] came into force. The 2021 Direction preserves the exclusion of "*any building the cubic content of which, measured externally, does not exceed 50 cubic metres*".[171] The 2021 Direction continues to provide[172] that building does not include "part of a building" so removing part of a building is not demolition for these purposes, and is likely to be seen as an alteration requiring planning permission. However it expressly excludes a "*statue, monument or memorial*" from "*demolition not to be taken to involve development of*

[166] *Sage v Secretary of State for the Environment, Transport and the Regions* [2003] UKHL 22, [2003] 2 All ER 689.

[167] Town and Country Planning Act 1990, s. 55(2)(g); a similar power is in the Planning Act (Northern Ireland) 2011, s. 23(3)(f).

[168] Town and Country Planning (Demolition – Description of Buildings) Direction 2014, §3(1)(a). I

[169] An exception would be Nelson's Column in Trafalgar Square. Some group memorials may also be larger than $50m^3$.

[170] The 2021 Direction was made by the Secretary of State pursuant to Town and Country Planning Act 1990, s. 55(2)(g).

[171] Paragraph 3(1)(a) of the 2021 Direction.

[172] Paragraph 2 of the 2021 Direction.

land"[173]. The purpose of the changes introduced by the 2021 Direction was to ensure that demolition of statues, memorials and monuments in England requires planning permission.[174]

The position in Wales is governed by the Welsh Demolition Direction 1995, which is contained in Annex A to Circular 10/95: Planning Controls over Demolition. The Welsh Direction excludes demolition of a ranges of categories of building from development. The exclusions include the demolition of any listed building, any building in a conservation area, any scheduled monument, and any building that is neither a dwelling nor adjoining a dwelling from the application of the Directive. In *R (Save Britain's Heritage) v Secretary of State for Communities and Local Government*[175] the Court of Appeal held that these exclusions in the then English Demolition Direction, which were in the same terms as the Welsh, were unlawful. The Welsh Direction has not been amended but the effect of the Court of Appeal decision is that the demolition of these buildings is not subject to a lawful direction for the purposes of s.55 and therefore requires planning permission.[176] The Court of Appeal decision did not consider the lawfulness of the exclusions concerning "any building whose volume is less than 50 cubic metres"[177] or "the whole or part of any gate, fence, wall or other means of enclosure (except those in a conservation area)".[178] The practical effect

173 Paragraph 3(2)(b) of the 2021 Direction.

174 The Background Note to the Direction explains that the 2021 Direction was introduced to ensure the demolition of statues, memorials and monuments in England requires permission pursuant to s.57(1) Town and Country Planning Act 1990. It was introduced at the same time as the Town and Country Planning (General Permitted Development etc.) (England) (Amendment) Order 2021 which excludes from the existing permitted development right the demolition of certain statues, memorials and monuments that have been in place for 10 years or more.

175 [2011] EWCA Civ 334 [2011] P.T.S.R. 1140.

176 A point immediately acknowledged in a letter from the Chief Planner to Welsh Chief Planning Officers, 18 April 2011.

177 The Welsh Demolition Direction, §2(1)(e).

178 The Welsh Demolition Direction, §2(1)(f).

is that the position in Wales is now the same as the position was in England prior to the introduction of the 2021 Direction.

In Northern Ireland the Planning (Demolition – Description of Buildings) Direction 2015 excludes from the definition of development the demolition or a structural alteration consisting of the partial demolition of any buildings of less than 115 m^3, gates, fences and walls.[179]

Applying those principles, the following analyses apply to whether planning permission is required to works affecting a heritage asset.

Heritage assets inside a building

If a heritage asset is part of a building (as opposed to a building in its own right) and located inside the building, then its removal will be an alteration affecting only the interior of the building and so will not be development.[180] It will not need planning permission unless there is a planning condition requiring its retention (a matter dealt with below).

Alterations or changes to a heritage asset which is fixed to the outside of a building or a building in its own right

If a heritage asset is part of a building, and located outside of the building, or a building in its own right, then the following analysis applies. The first question is whether the alteration amounts to a building or other operation. As noted above, building operations including "*structural alterations of or additions to buildings*" and other operations normally undertaken by a builder. Whether something amounts to a structural alteration or an operation normally undertaken by a builder is a question of fact and degree. The second question is whether the alteration materially affects the external appearance of the building. This is a question of planning judgement.

---

[179] Except for walls in designated areas of townscape or village characters.

[180] Town and Country Planning Act 1990, s.55(2)(1); Planning Act (Northern Ireland) 2011, s.23(3)(a).

Again, there is limited assistance in the case law as to how these questions will be applied in practice to heritage assets. The reported cases indicate that a broad approach will be taken to the meaning of building operations for the purposes of s.55.

a. In *Bradford Metropolitan District Council v Secretary of State for the Environment*[181] cladding a red-brick house with stone tiles was found to constitute development for the purposes of s.55 TCPA but permitted on the basis that it fell within the scope of permitted development rights.

b. In *Windsor and Maidenhead RBC v Secretary of State for the Environment*[182] Mann J held that repainting a Grade II listed terrace house could constitute an alteration, and therefore development for the purposes of s.55. The painting and repainting of the building being an operation normally undertaken by a person carrying on business as a builder.

c. In *Kensington and Chelsea RBC v C.G. Hotels*[183] the question was whether the installation of floodlights at the ground and first-floor levels of a hotel constituted development. Donaldson LJ proceeded on the assumption that running electric cables and placing floodlights in position could constitute development for the purposes of the legislative predecessor to s.55 TCPA,[184] but that this work did not materially affect the external appearance of the building.

d. In *Westminster City Council v Verjee*[185] the inspector held that fixing festoon lighting to a hotel in Bayswater constituted development which materially affected the external appearance of the building. In reaching this conclusion, the inspector noted that the lighting was not confined to a small part of the building

[181] [1977] 10 WLUK 64, (1978) 35 P & CR 387.

[182] [1987] 12 WLUK 295; (1988) 56 P & CR 427.

[183] [1980] 10 WLUK 180, (1981) 41 P & CR 40.

[184] Town and Country Planning Act 1971, s. 22(1).

[185] [1992] 5 WLUK 224, (1992) 7 PAD 572.

but ran vertically and horizontally against both facades of the building. It was also permanently attached to the fabric of the original building, the festoon comprising light bulbs and holders, black plastic sheathed cable and junction boxes at periodic intervals.

These cases suggest the following analysis of situations which may arise in relation to heritage assets:

a. It will depend on the circumstances whether or not the removal, or addition, of a plaque from a statue or other heritage asset would constitute a building operation so as to be capable of development. Depending on the nature of affixation, removal might well be a straightforward operation capable of being undertaken without the assistance of a builder, although any need to make good what it was attached to would have to be taken into account,. Whether or not the removal or attachment of a plaque materially affected the external appearance of the building would also depend on its prominence having regard to factors such as size, location and colour.

b. Painting or repainting may be a building operation so as to be capable of development. This might depend on the nature of painting or repainting. In *Windsor and Maidenhead RBC* it was relevant that painting of the type of building in question was found to be an operation normally undertaken by a person carrying on business as a builder. It is not clear that the same would be said of painting or repainting a statue or monument. Defacing a statue or monument through graffiti could not be described as an operation normally undertaken by a person carrying on business as a builder and so is unlikely to constitute development.

c. Restoration work or cleaning to an artistic feature in *situ* might constitute development, but it is a question of the scale and effect of the works. It would first have to amount to a building or other operation, and then materially affect the external appearance of the building. Routine cleaning and touching up is not likely to need planning permission.

Removal of a heritage asset which is fixed to the outside of a building

Where a heritage asset forms part of a building, for example a statue attached to the exterior of a building or a statue on a plinth, its removal (whether for relocation or destruction) is likely to constitute development. This is because removal of the heritage asset is likely to constitute a "structural alteration" to the building, so as to constitute a building operation. The nature and degree or annexation, and therefore whether building operations are required for removal of the asset, may also be relevant to whether removal constitutes development. A distinction may be drawn between a small statue affixed to a building with screws, which can easily be removed, and a statue attached by cement or other adhesive, removal of which is likely to involve work of a nature that is usually carried out a builder and is more likely to alter the structure of the building.

If removal of a heritage asset from the exterior of a building involves development, it will need planning permission if the removal materially affects the external appearance of the building.[186] Whether removal of a heritage asset materially affects the external appearance of the building is a question of planning judgement. For example, removal of a large statute affixed to a building would likely materially affect the external appearance of the building. However, removal of a plaque might not material affect the external appearance of the building.

Removal of a heritage asset which is a building in its own right

Previously, most heritage assets would have fallen within the exemption covering demolition "*any building the cubic content of which, measured externally, does not exceed 50 cubic metres*".[187] Following the entry into force of the Town and Country Planning (Demolition – Description of Buildings) Direction 2021, statues, monuments and memorials are excluded from this exemption. It follows that demolition of most heritage

[186] Town and Country Planning Act 1990, s. 55(2)(a); Planning Act (Northern Ireland) 2011, s. 23(3)(a).

[187] Town and Country Planning (Demolition – Description of Buildings) Direction 2014. Most heritage assets are less than 50 m^3. An exception would be Nelson's Column in Trafalgar Square, which is just over 50 m in height.

assets which are listed as buildings in their own right will require planning permission.

The position in relation to relocation of heritage assets, for example to a museum, is uncertain. The first issue that would arise is whether relocation constitutes demolition. If it constitutes demolition then it is development for the purposes of s.55 TCPA.[188] In *Shimizu (UK) Ltd v Westminster City Council*[189], the House of Lords held that whether or not there is demolition of a building for the purposes of the Planning (Listed Buildings and Conservation Areas) Act 1990 is a question of fact and degree to be assessed on a quantitative basis, i.e. by reference to the extent of demolition.[190] Removing a heritage asset from its location is likely to involve demolition where there is dismantling. This conclusion finds support in the judgment of Sullivan J in *Judge v First Secretary of State*.[191] The case concerned the grant of listed building consent to relocate a Grade II listed statue of Sir Samuel Sadler from one position in Victoria Square in Middlesborough town centre to a new location in Victoria Square. The consent was challenged on the basis that listed building consent could only be given for the demolition of a listed building, not its relocation. Sullivan J held that "relocate" had been used as a shorthand for describing the process of demolition followed by reconstruction on another site. The removal of the statue, which involved a process of dismantling the statue from its plinth and the surrounding semi-circular wall (both of which formed part of the listing), constituted demolition. The re-erection of the statue, plinth and wall, some months later, at the

---

188 This is the effect of s.55 (1A)(a) TCPA which defines "building operations" as including demolition of buildings.

189 [1997] 1 WLR 168.

190 [1997] 1 WLR 168 at pp 185F–H, 186C and 187B, followed in *Walter Lilly & Co Ltd v Clin* [2021] EWCA Civ 136 [2021] 1 WLR 2753 at §76. This case is considered in detail in Chapter 2 above.

191 [2005] EWHC 887 (Admin). This decision is also considered in Chapter 2 above. Permission to appeal to the Court of Appeal was refused [2005] EWCA Civ 1155. Refusing leave to appeal, Buxton L.J. held that: "*True it is, of course, that the code in terms does not deal with the moving of a building. But I find it impossible to say that such a step is excluded from the code--that is to say, excluded from any possibility of receiving listed building permission--merely by the fact that an object of this sort is to be moved rather than left in its place*".

new location constituted reconstruction. The position is less clear where a heritage asset can be removed without any dismantling or other buildings operations. In *Dill*, Lord Carnwath stated that "*works for the demolition*" "*clearly envisages some form of dismantling (i.e. "pulling down or taking to pieces" in the words of Jenkins J in the Cardiff case*[192]*) when the item is removed from the site*".[193] This would support the conclusion that where a heritage asset can be removed without any dismantling or other building operation there will be no demolition.

If removal or relocation does not constitute demolition, then the question will be whether the act of relocating the asset involves a building operation. For large, heavy assets, relocation may well involve work which would constitute "building operations" for the purposes of s.55 TCPA. For example, the need to involve machinery such as a crane or hoist[194], or the time and complexity of work involved[195], might support a conclusion that removal involves building operations or engineering operations, all of which constitute development. For smaller, or lighter, assets, which can be removed without the need for machinery or other works which could constitute "building operations", it is unlikely that relocation will constitute development. In these cases, planning permission would not be required.

Are there permitted development rights?

Where proposed works to a heritage asset require planning permission, permitted development rights may apply. It is important to note that permitted development rights only grant planning permission. They do not affect the need for other consents, such as those required in relation

---

192 *Cardiff Rating Authority v Guest Keen Baldwin's Iron and Steel Co Ltd* [1949] 1 KB 385.

193 *Dill* at §53.

194 In *Dill,* at §58, Lord Carnwath stated that the fact that the urns required a small crane to move them provided some support for the conclusion that the items were buildings.

195 In *Hall Hunter Partnership* (the polytunnel case) Sullivan J considered the fact that it would take over 300 hours to dismantle the polytunnels supported his conclusion that the polytunnels were buildings.

to a listed building or scheduled monument, or the need to obtain conservation area consent.

As the concept of development is wide, the TCPA provides that the Secretary of State may issue orders granting planning permission for certain operations and use.[196] Permitted development rights are set out in the Town and Country Planning (General Permitted Development) (England) Order 2015 ("the GDPO"), as amended, the Town and Country Planning (General Permitted Development) Order 1995 in Wales and the Planning (General Permitted Development) Order (Northern Ireland) 2015.

There are two categories of permitted development right which may be relevant to works to heritage assets which are attached to buildings are buildings in their own right:

a. Permitted development rights granting planning permission for alteration to buildings

There are extensive permitted development rights which automatically grant planning permission for alterations to buildings. These permitted development rights may be relevant to a modest number of heritage assets and are summarised below for completeness. Removing a work of art from the exterior of a house is likely to be covered by rights to alter dwellinghouses. Installing such a work is more problematic as there are restrictions on extending the house beyond certain walls and "*the materials used in any exterior work (other than materials used in the construction of a conservatory) must be of a similar appearance to those used in the construction of the exterior of the existing dwellinghouse*".[197] Permitted development rights for extensions to roofs are more limited, so the Headington Shark, a 7.6 metre long fibreglass sculpture shown

[196] Town and Country Planning Act 1990, s. 58(1) and ss.59-61.

[197] Altering dwellinghouses is permitted by Town and Country Planning (General Permitted Development) (England) Order 2015, Schedule 2, Part 1, Class A; Town and Country Planning (General Permitted Development) Order 1995, Schedule 2, Part 1, Class A; Planning (General Permitted Development) Order (Northern Ireland) 2015, Schedule 2, Part 1, Class A. In these householder permitted development rights, dwellinghouse does not include a building containing flats.

plunging headfirst into the roof of a terraced house in Oxford, was not permitted development.[198] There are extensive permitted development rights to provide within the curtilage of a dwellinghouse any building "*required for a purpose incidental to the enjoyment of the dwellinghouse as such*".[199] These would include the installation of artworks (if they required planning permission) provided that they are for the appreciation of the house's residents or for its enhancement. Various limits on the right may be relevant, in that the building may not be forward of the principal elevation, higher than 2.5 metres within 2 metres of the boundary of the curtilage or higher than 3 metres otherwise, or within the curtilage of a listed building.[200]

Commercial and institutional use permitted development rights include the alteration of office buildings at ground floor level[201] and the alteration of a school, college, university or hospital building which is not within five metres of the boundary of the curtilage of the premises.[202] It should be noted that a Council's main building, with the council chamber and committee rooms, might not be an office because of its characteristics for public debate and decision making.[203] Statutory undertakers, including railway companies have extensive permitted development rights which

[198] At 2 New High Street, Headington, Oxford. The sculpture, by John Buckley, was installed in 1986. After being the subject of enforcement action, planning permission was granted on appeal by the Secretary of State

[199] Town and Country Planning (General Permitted Development) (England) Order 2015, Schedule 2, Part 1, Class E; Town and Country Planning (General Permitted Development) Order 1995, Schedule 2, Part 1, Class E; Planning (General Permitted Development) Order (Northern Ireland) 2015, Schedule 2, Part 1, Class D.

[200] The Northern Irish exceptions are slightly different.

[201] Town and Country Planning (General Permitted Development) (England) Order 2015, Schedule 2, Part 7, Class F. Similar provisions apply in Wales and Northern Ireland.

[202] Town and Country Planning (General Permitted Development) (England) Order 2015, Schedule 2, Part 7, Class M.

[203] *London Residuary Body v London Borough of Lambeth* (1989) 58 P & CR 370.

could include the removal of statues.[204] Local authorities do have permitted development rights to alter small ancillary buildings required for the purpose of any function exercised by them on the land or various structures such as lamp standards, public shelters and seats.[205] These permitted development rights are unlikely to apply to most public statues. More generally, the painting of the exterior of any building or work is permitted development except when it is for the purpose of advertisement, announcement or direction.[206] Where permitted development rights apply then no planning application will need to be made.

b. Permitted development rights granting planning permission for demolition of buildings

In England planning permission is granted by permitted development rights for the demolition of a building[207] (but not part of a building).[208] In England and Wales the demolition of a whole building is not permitted by any other permitted development rights than those specific to demolition. .[209]

---

204 Town and Country Planning (General Permitted Development) (England) Order 2015, Schedule 2, Parts 8, 13, 15, albeit these rights do not include the demolition of a building: GPDO art 3(9).

205 Town and Country Planning (General Permitted Development) (England) Order 2015, Schedule 2, Part 12, Class A.

206 Town and Country Planning (General Permitted Development) (England) Order 2015, Schedule 2, Part 2, Class C; Town and Country Planning (General Permitted Development) Order 1995, Schedule 2, Part 2, Class C; Planning (General Permitted Development) Order (Northern Ireland) 2015, Schedule 2, Part 3, Class C.

207 Town and Country Planning (General Permitted Development) (England) Order 2015, Schedule 2 Part 11, Class B. Town and Country Planning (General Permitted Development) Order 1995, Schedule 2, Part 31, Class A; Planning (General Permitted Development) Order (Northern Ireland) 2015, Schedule 2, Part 33, Class A.

208 Town and Country Planning (General Permitted Development) (England) Order 2015, art. 2(1).

209 Town and Country Planning (General Permitted Development) (England) Order 2015, art. 3(9); Town and Country Planning (General Permitted Development) Order 1995, art. 3(9). There is no similar exception in Northern Ireland.

There are, however, exceptions to these permitted development rights, with different exceptions applying in England, Wales and Northern Ireland.

In England Part 11, Class B authorises the demolition of a building. The exceptions in England are as follows: the building has been rendered unsafe or otherwise uninhabitable by the action or inaction of any person having an interest in the land on which the building stands and it is practicable to secure safety or health by works of repair or works for affording temporary support; the demolition is relevant demolition in a conservation area[210]; the building was last used as a pub; the building was last used as a concert hall, live music venue or theatre; or the demolition relates to a statue, memorial or monument in place for a period of at least 10 years on the date of any proposed demolition.[211] The last exception was added by the Town and Country Planning (General Permitted Development etc.) (England) (Amendment) Order 2021/428 and aims to afford additional protection to certain commemorative structures which have been in place for more than ten years. In all of these cases, development is not permitted by the GDPO.

Unless additionally authorised by another process,[212] demolition under Part 11, Class B has to go through a prior approval process for the method of demolition and any proposed restoration of the site. An application for a prior approval determination must be made to the local planning authority with a written description of the proposed development and confirmation of a site notice display.[213] The applicant is required to display a site notice, allowing representations to be made

---

[210] For the purposes of the Town and Country Planning Act 1990, s.196D.

[211] Town and Country Planning (General Permitted Development) (England) Order 2015, Schedule 2 Part 11, Class B, para B1.

[212] A prior approval determination is not required for excluded demolition, which is demolition on land already subject to a planning permission for redevelopment, demolition authorised by listed building or scheduled monument consent, required or permitted to be carried out by or under any other enactment or required to be carried out under a planning obligation: Town and Country Planning (General Permitted Development) (England) Order 2015, Schedule 2 Part 11, Class B, § B3.

[213] Town and Country Planning (General Permitted Development) (England) Order 2015, Schedule 2 Part 11, Class B, condition B2(b)(ii).

to the local authority. Prescribed or model forms are not available, so care needs to be taken in drafting the site notice. A failure to comply with the notice requirements is a breach of condition preventing the permitted development right arising. A site display means "*the posting of the notice by firmly attaching it to some object, sited and displayed in such a way as to be easily visible and legible by members of the public*".[214] The local planning authority must either give notice that prior approval is not required, prior approval is required and refused or prior approval is granted within 28 days from the receipt of the application.[215] If notice is not given then the applicant can proceed in accordance with the submission.

The English Part 11, Class C authorises the demolition of the whole or any part of any gate, fence, wall or other means of enclosure, unless it is relevant demolition in a conservation area.[216] Similar rights exist in Wales, but without a conservation area exclusion.[217]

Part 31, Class A authorises the demolition of buildings in Wales. the only exclusion is where a building has been rendered unsafe or uninhabitable, by the action or inaction of anyone having an interest in the land on which the building stands and it is practicable to secure safety or health by works of repair or works for affording temporary support.[218] A prior approval process is required.

---

214 Town and Country Planning (General Permitted Development) (England) Order 2015, art 2(1); Town and Country Planning (General Permitted Development) Order 1995, art 1(2). So, for example, a notice of demolition fixed to a rear door of Carham Hall, over 200 metres away from and on the opposite side of the building to the road was not valid: *R (on the application of SAVE Britain's Heritage) v Northumberland County Council* (2021) (submission to judgment).

215 Town and Country Planning (General Permitted Development) (England) Order 2015, Schedule 2 Part 11, Class B, condition B2(b)(vii).

216 Town and Country Planning (General Permitted Development) (England) Order 2015, Schedule 2 Part 11, Class C.

217 Town and Country Planning (General Permitted Development) Order 1995, Schedule 2, Part 31, Class B

218 Town and Country Planning (General Permitted Development) Order 1995, Schedule 2, Part 31, Class A.

In Northern Ireland a single class, Part 33, Class A authorises the demolition of buildings, including walls and other means of enclosure. Permitted development rights for demolition are excluded in areas of townscape character or an area of village character.[219] In Wales and Northern Ireland, demolition in conservation areas is controlled by conservation area consent.

The prior approval process is not itself capable of stopping demolition, if the application is made properly, but it does impose a pause. That may be used by the local planning authority to withdraw permitted development rights by an Article 4 direction, or by the Minister to list the building.

A local planning authority or the Secretary of State may remove specified permitted development rights in an area or for a particular development by making an Article 4 Direction.[220] Compensation is payable by the local authority for any loss caused by an Article 4 Direction if planning permission is subsequently refused.[221]

Demolition or alteration in breach of planning conditions

There will be some circumstances where the placing and retention of heritage assets, such as statues or other works of art, is required by a condition on a planning permission.[222] In such cases planning permission, or possibly an approval under the condition, would be required for their removal or replacement.

---

219 Unless required by certain statutory provisions: Planning (General Permitted Development) Order (Northern Ireland) 2015, Schedule 2, Part 33, Class A, § A1.

220 Town and Country Planning (General Permitted Development) (England) Order 2015, art. 4. Town and Country Planning (General Permitted Development) Order 1995, art. 4.

221 Town and Country Planning Act 1990, s. 108. This may be significant if the statue would have greater value as a chattel detached from the site.

222 These would tend to be at large commercial or residential schemes constructed in the last 30-40 years.

Historically the Arts Council had a 'Percentage for Art', for developers to spend 1% of the costs on public art at the site. This has not been reflected in national planning policy, although it has been found in some form in some local planning policies. Public art can undoubtedly be part of a good design.

If the public art is seen as essential to the acceptability of the development then a condition might be imposed on the planning permission to secure that an artwork is installed and maintained in place. Such a condition might allow the artwork to be changed with the approval of the local planning authority. Such an approval would have to be sought by an application in writing and can be appealed to the Minister if refused or not determined.

An example is the construction of the Montague Shopping Centre, Worthing, under a 1987 planning permission. The rear of the shopping centre would back onto Liverpool Gardens which contains open space and an 1830s listed terrace. To soften the otherwise unattractive back of the scheme, a sculpture commissioned from Dame Elisabeth Frink was proposed on a loggia. The Desert Quartet comprised four monumental bronze cast sculptured heads, each mounted and displayed on a pier. Conditions on the planning permission required the permanent siting of the work. A planning application to remove the Desert Quartet and replace them with a less valuable work was refused in 2002.[223] When further proposals to relocate the sculptures came forward in the Desert Quartet, their piers and the loggia were listed at grade II*.[224]

[223] Appeal reference APP/M3835/A/02/1083723.

[224] A discussion and photograph of the Desert Quartet is in Historic England's *Commemorative Structures Listing Selection Guide.*

Applying for planning permission

In brief, applications for planning permission must almost always be made to the relevant local planning authority.[225]

Historic England have to be consulted on planning applications which involve demolition, in whole or in part, or the material alteration of a listed building which is classified as grade I or grade II* or which are likely to affect the site of a scheduled monument.[226] They must also be consulted on planning applications which would affect the setting of a grade I or II* listed building.[227]

Planning applications are decided by planning committees of councillors or by officers under delegated powers. A planning application is finally determined when the decision notice is sent out by the local planning authority.

The national authorities are able to 'call-in' applications for their own determination prior to the issue of a decision by the local authority.[228] To do that, the Minister needs to know of the application. Another part of the 2021 contested heritage provisions in England was to require the local planning authority to refer any commemorative object planning application to the Secretary of State unless they were proposing to refuse it. The Town and Country Planning (Consultation) (England) Direction

---

225 For an introduction to the planning regime see Richard Harwood, *Planning Permission* (Bloomsbury Professional, 2016). For an overview of the planning application process see Richard Harwood, *Historic Environment Law* (Institute of Art and Law 2012) chapter 9.

226 Town and Country Planning (Development Management Procedure) (England) Order 2015, Schedule 18, § (q) and (r). The effect on the scheduled monument must be direct: see *R(Williams) v Powys County Council* [2017] EWCA Civ 427 at §§ 31 to 35 per Lindblom LJ where 'likely to affect the site of a scheduled monument' does not include an effect only on its setting.

227 Planning (Listed Buildings and Conservation Areas) Regulations 1990, SI 1990/1519, reg 5A(3).

228 Town and Country Planning Act 1990, s. 77.

2021[229] was brought into force for planning applications received on or after that date. In this Direction:[230]

> *""commemorative object development" means development which consists of or includes full or part demolition of a statue, monument, memorial or plaque which is, or is part of, a building in place for a period of at least 10 years on the date of any proposed demolition other than a statue, monument, memorial or plaque:*
>
> *(a) that is a listed building;*
>
> *(b) that is a scheduled monument;*
>
> *(c) within a cemetery, on consecrated land, or within the curtilage of a place of public worship;*
>
> *(d) within the grounds of a museum or art gallery; or*
>
> *(e) within the curtilage of a dwellinghouse".*

The first three exceptions reflect alternative consent regimes, the first two of which do or may end up with the Minister. The exceptions for museums and art galleries reflect the potentially transient nature of a display and for dwellinghouses are concerned with their private nature. Statues and similar items might be listed in such contexts. By paragraph 10 of the Direction:

> *"Where a local planning authority does not propose to refuse an application for planning permission to which this Direction applies, the authority shall consult the Secretary of State".*

The Secretary of State would normally be consulted after the local planning authority have decided that they would wish to approve the application, with a copy of representations received and any officer report being provided.[231] The planning application may not be determined

---

[229] Town and Country Planning (Consultation) (England) Direction 2021, § 1.

[230] Town and Country Planning (Consultation) (England) Direction 2021, § 9.

[231] Town and Country Planning (Consultation) (England) Direction 2021, § 11.

within 21 days of referral, unless the Minister agrees.[232] This period may be extended by the Minister making an Article 31 Direction[233] to prohibit the grant of planning permission for a further period or indefinitely, but in practice pending a decision whether to call in the application.

The applicant for a planning permission has a right of appeal to the Secretary of State for Levelling Up, Housing and Communities (in England), the Welsh Ministers (in Wales) or the Planning Appeals Commission (in Northern Ireland) against refusal of an application, its grant subject to conditions or non-determination of the application. Appeals are usually determined by a planning inspector unless recovered by the Secretary of State or Welsh Ministers, or by a Commissioner in Northern Ireland. They may be determined following written representations, following a hearing or following a public inquiry. Planning decisions may be challenged in the High Court either by judicial review or statutory application or appeal.[234]

Conclusions on the need for planning applications in respect of heritage assets

In summary, the following analysis would apply to works affecting the following types of heritage assets.

Assets which are part of larger structures, such as statues fixed outside buildings, or plaques

[232] Town and Country Planning (Consultation) (England) Direction 2021, § 12, 13.

[233] Under the Town and Country Planning (Development Management Procedure) (England) Order 2015, art. 31; Town and Country Planning (Development Management Procedure) (Wales) Order 2012, art. 18; Planning (General Development Procedure) Order (Northern Ireland) 2015, art. 17.

[234] An application to the High Court may be brought against the Secretary of State or Inspector's decisions on planning appeals or call-ins under Town and Country Planning Act 1990, s.288. An appeal may be brought against a decision of the Secretary of State or Inspector on an enforcement notice appeal, under Town and Country Planning Act 1990, s.289.

Planning permission would be required for the removal of, or alteration to, a statue or plaque on the exterior of a building, provided it is part of the building and the alteration materially affects the external appearance of the building and does not benefit from permitted development rights.

Planning permission would be required for any alteration or demolition which is contrary to a condition on a planning permission which is in effect on the site.

Statues on plinths or other bases

Planning permission would be required for the removal of a statue or plaque which is fixed to a substantial plinth, provided the plinth remains and, in the case of a plaque, the alteration materially affects the external appearance of the building.

Planning permission would also be required for any alteration or demolition which is contrary to a condition on a planning permission which is in effect on the site.

Freestanding statues

Items which are not fixed to a building (in a property law sense of the degree and purpose of annexation) or which are not buildings in their own right (considering size, permanence and degree of attachment) are not subject to planning or listed building control at all. Similarly items which are inside buildings will not be subject to planning control.

CHAPTER THREE

SCHEDULED MONUMENTS AND CONSERVATION AREAS

Previous chapters have addressed the need for planning permission and listed building consent in order to carry out works affecting heritage assets. The two planning related regimes which may apply to workings affecting heritage assets are:

a. scheduled monument consent;

b. conservation area consent.

Scheduled Monuments

The Ancient Monuments and Archaeological Areas Act 1979 gives protection to "*scheduled monuments*". A monument is scheduled if it is designated by the Secretary of State or the Welsh Ministers as being of national importance.[235] In Northern Ireland the Department can schedule "*such monuments as it thinks fit*".[236]

Heritage assets may be designated as scheduled monuments or, occasionally, be located within the area covered by a scheduled monument. By section 61(7) of the Ancient Monuments and Archaeological Areas Act 1979, a "monument" is:[237]

a. any building, structure or work, whether above or below the surface of the land, and any cave or excavation;

---

[235] Ancient Monuments and Archaeological Areas Act 1979, s. 1.

[236] Historic Monuments and Archaeological Objects (Northern Ireland) Order 1995, art. 3(1).

[237] Ancient Monuments and Archaeological Areas Act 1979, s. 61(7); Historic Monuments and Archaeological Objects (Northern Ireland) Order 1995, art. 2(6).

b. any site comprising its remains;

c. any site comprising any vehicle, vessel, aircraft or other movable structure or part or its remains.

Historic England maintains a searchable database of all scheduled monuments in England.[238] However, care needs to be taken. A scheduled monument is therefore the monument itself, the site of the monument (being the land in or on which it is situated) and land "*comprising or adjoining it*" that the Secretary of State considers is "*essential for the monument's support and preservation*" and has included in the Schedule. The scheduled monument is whatever is within the schedule entry which usually includes a boundary drawn on a plan. This may include structures which are not themselves the monument, including later installed heritage assets. In 2006 it was reported that a cast iron balustrade installed by Princess Margaret in the garden at Kensington Palace was withdrawn from auction because it was caught by the scheduling of the Palace.[239]

Scheduling entries will sometimes exclude particular items or types or items. For example the schedule entry for Winchester Castle (which is principally Roman and medieval remains) excludes modern buildings, structures, posts and specifically the statue of Napoleonic War hero Sir John Colborne.

Scheduled monument consent is required for:[240]

> *"(a) any works resulting in the demolition or destruction of or any damage to a scheduled monument;*
>
> *(b) any works for the purpose of removing or repairing a scheduled monument or any part of it or of making any alterations or additions thereto; and*

---

[238] https://historicengland.org.uk/listing/the-list/

[239] '£15m richer, Lord Linley gives the nation a balustrade', *The Guardian*, 15 June 2006.

[240] Ancient Monuments and Archaeological Areas Act 1979, s. 2; Historic Monuments and Archaeological Objects (Northern Ireland) Order 1995, art. 4(1).

(c) any flooding or tipping operations on land in, on or under which there is a scheduled monument."

This is a more extensive form of control than planning permission, which is required for works if they materially affect the external appearance of a building, and listing building control, which is only required if works affect the special architectural or historic interest of the particular building. So whilst scheduled monument issues arise infrequently in the context of statues, care needs to be taken.

Conservation Areas

Conservation areas are "*areas of special architectural or historic interest the character or appearance of which it is desirable to preserve or enhance*" which have been designated, usually by local authorities.[241] These will often include historic town centres or urban parks where memorials and statues may be found. Some tightened controls apply which may have an effect on those objects.

Historically, conservation area consent was required for the demolition of most unlisted buildings in conservation areas in England, Wales and Northern Ireland. In 2013 conservation area consent was abolished in England, but all such "*relevant demolition*" requires planning permission and unlike other planning matters, breaches are subject to immediate criminal liability.

For the purposes of conservation area consent and relevant demolition in Wales and England respectively, the demolition needs to be of substantially the whole building. The *Shimizu*[242] test for the demolition of a listed building is applied to these conservation area concepts.[243]

---

[241] Planning (Listed Buildings and Conservation Areas) Act 1990, s. 69; Planning Act (Northern Ireland) 2011, s. 104.

[242] *Shimizu (UK) Ltd v Westminster City Council* [1997] 1 WLR 168.

[243] *Walter Lilly & Co v Clin* [2021] EWCA Civ 136, [2021] 1 W.L.R. 2753 at §§ 51 to 59 per Carr LJ, applying *Shimizu (UK) Ltd v Westminster City Council* [1997] 1 WLR 168.

Conservation Areas in England

In England, it is a criminal offence to carry out "*relevant demolition*" in a conservation area without planning permission or in breach of a condition on a planning permission.[244] Relevant demolition uses as the same provisions as the scope of conservation area consent. Consequently it is the demolition of a building in a conservation area[245]and which is not excluded under the Planning (Listed Buildings and Conservation Areas) Act 1990 ("Listed Buildings Act 1990"), s. 75. Section 75 excludes listed buildings, ecclesiastical buildings which are used for ecclesiastical purposes, scheduled monuments and buildings in relation to which a direction has been made by the Secretary of State.[246]

The Conservation Areas Direction 2015[247] was made under s. 75 and excludes from the relevant demolition category a number of categories of buildings including "*any building with a total cubic content not exceeding 115 cubic metres (as ascertained by external measurement) or any part of such a building, other than a pre-1925 tombstone*".[248] The 115 m^3 limit is less restrictive than the 50 m^3 minimum size in the Demolition Direction, so the demolition of statues caught by it would have needed planning permission in any event. The tombstone provision is more important. As defined in the Conservation Areas Direction, a "*pre-1925 tombstone*" means "*a monument or memorial to a deceased person which was erected before 1 January 1925*". Notwithstanding the reference to tombstone, the monument or memorial need not be at the individual's grave nor in a churchyard or cemetery. Consequently it would include a statue in a public square which was erected prior to 1925 for historic (and then deceased) benefactors. Permitted development rights do not

244 Town and Country Planning Act 1990, s.196D(1) and (2).

245 Planning (Listed Buildings and Conservation Areas) Act 1990 ('the Listed Buildings Act 1990'), s. 74(1).

246 Planning (Listed Buildings and Conservation Areas) Act 1990, s. 75(1).

247 The Conservation Areas (Application of Section 74 of the Planning (Listed Buildings and Conservation Areas) Act 1990) Direction 2015 made pursuant to the Planning (Listed Buildings and Conservation Areas) Act 1990, s. 75(2).

248 Other exceptions relate to buildings which have to be demolished under other powers.

authorise "*relevant demolition*" so an application for planning permission would be required to authorise the removal of such statues.

Historic England must be consulted when a local planning authority makes a planning application to itself for relevant demolition.[249] If the application is solely for relevant demolition in a conservation area then the application shall be sent to the Secretary of State for determination if Historic England objects.[250]

Conservation Areas in Wales

Pursuant to s. 74 of the Listed Buildings Act 1990, conservation area consent is required for the demolition of buildings in conservation areas in Wales, subject to the exclusions in or made under s. 75 (set out above).[251] Pre-1925 tombstones are subject to the requirement for conservation area consent, however the Welsh direction which sets this out omits the definition.[252]

Conservation Areas in Northern Ireland

In Northern Ireland, conservation area consent is required for the demolition of all unlisted buildings in conservation areas except for ecclesiastical buildings, scheduled monuments[253] and those which are the subject of the Planning (Northern Ireland) Act 2011 Planning (Control of Demolition in Conservation Areas) Direction 2015.[254] The concept of demolition is widened to include "*any structural alteration of that*

[249] Town and Country Planning General Regulations 1992, reg 4A(1).

[250] Town and Country Planning General Regulations 1992, reg 4A.

[251] Listed Buildings Act, s. 74.

[252] Conservation Areas (Disapplication of requirement for Conservation Area Consent for Demolition) (Wales) Direction (2017 No. 27). The previous direction in paragraph 20 of Welsh Office Circular 01/98 did use the same definition as in England, but that has been cancelled.

[253] See Planning Act (Northern Ireland) 2011, s. 85(8) for the ecclesiastical and scheduled monument exceptions.

[254] Planning Act (Northern Ireland) 2011, s. 105(1), (2).

building where the alteration consists of demolishing part of the building"[255] and so would include removing a statue from a plinth if the assemblage qualified. However the minimum size is 115 m^3 and there is no protection for tombstones.

Conclusions on the need for conservation area consent or scheduled monument consent

In summary, the following analysis would apply to works affecting the following types of heritage assets.

a. Assets which are part of larger structures, such as statues fixed outside buildings, or plaques.

b. Statues on plinths or other bases.

c. Freestanding statutes.

Scheduled monument consent

If the heritage asset forms part of a larger structure, and that structure is designated as a scheduled monument, or if the heritage asset is located within the area covered by a scheduled monument, work affecting the asset will require scheduled monument consent. It is important to bear in mind that the scheduled monument is whatever is within the schedule entry which usually includes a boundary drawn on a plan and that this may include structures which are not themselves the monument, including later installed heritage assets.

Conservation area consent

In England, if a heritage asset is located within a conservation area, is unlisted but constitutes a building in its own right, demolition will require planning permission if the asset is larger than 115 m^3. Likewise, if the asset – such as a plaque or statue – is fixed to a building larger than 115 m^3 its removal will require planning permission. Planning

[255] Planning Act (Northern Ireland) 2011, s. 105(8).

permission will also be required for demolition of an asset which is a monument or memorial to a deceased person and was erected before 1925. This could include assets (such as plaques) attached to larger structures as well as statues.

In Wales and Northern Ireland, if a heritage asset is located within a conservation area, is unlisted but constitutes a building in its own right, conservation area consent will require planning permission if the asset is larger than 115 m^3. If the asset – such as a plaque or statue – is fixed to a building larger than 115 m^3 its removal will require conservation area consent.

CHAPTER FOUR

GRANT OF REGULATORY CONSENT

The determination of an application for planning permission, listed building consent, conservation area consent or scheduled monument consent are exercises of discretion. That discretion must be exercised accordance with the relevant statutory provisions and having regard to relevant policy.

This chapter provides an overview of considerations which must be taken into account when making decisions affecting heritage assets. Although considerations vary across different regulatory regimes, the following matters will generally need to be taken into account:

a. Mandatory considerations stipulated in legislation;

b. National policy;

c. Other relevant and material considerations, which may include local policies;

d. Equalities duties.

Certain heritage assets have generated controversy due to their association with historical iniquities. This is particularly the case in respect of statues and memorials to historical figures or events associated with the slave trade. Public discourse about what to do with such contested heritage has included calls for them to be removed, but there is disagreement as to whether that is the right course of action. The final section of this chapter considers how these issues may be relevant to the determination of applications for regulatory consent.

Statutory provisions

The Planning (Listed Buildings and Conservation Areas) Act 1990 ("the Listed Buildings Act 1990") sets out a number of mandatory considerations which apply to the determination of applications to de-list a building and for listed building consent, planning permission and conservation area consent.

On an application to de-list a building, the Secretary of State must be satisfied that the building no longer meets the statutory criteria for a building being included on the list, i.e. that it holds special architectural or historic interest. When it comes to applications for listed buildings consent, there is a strong statutory presumption that listed buildings will be preserved.[256] Section 16(2) of the Listed Buildings Act 1990 imposes a duty when determining listed building consent applications:

> *"In considering whether to grant listed building consent for any works the local planning authority or the Secretary of State shall have special regard to the desirability of preserving the building or its setting or any features of special architectural or historic interest which it possesses."*

Section 66(1) of the Listed Buildings Act 1990 applies a similar duty in relation to listed buildings to the determination of planning applications:

> *"In considering whether to grant planning permission or permission in principle for development which affects a listed building or its setting, the local planning authority or, as the case may be, the Secretary of State shall have special regard to the desirability of preserving the building or its setting or any features of special architectural or historic interest which it possesses."*

Controls are less strict where buildings are not listed or scheduled. There is a similar statutory presumption in favour of preserving or enhancing the character or appearance of a conservation area in England and Wales.

---

[256] Listed Buildings Act, s. 66 as explained by *East Northamptonshire District Council v Secretary of State for Communities and Local Government* [2014] EWCA Civ 137, [2014] 1 P & CR 22.

This is set out in s. 72(1) of the Listed Buildings Act 1990 which provides:[257]

> *"In the exercise, with respect to any buildings or other land in a conservation area, of any functions under or by virtue of any of the provisions mentioned in subsection (2), special attention shall be paid to the desirability of preserving or enhancing the character or appearance of that area."*

This gives rise to a strong presumption that any application which fails to preserve this should be refused.[258] An even stronger presumption in Northern Ireland towards enhancing that character or appearance.[259] A presumption can of course be overcome, even where it attaches considerable weight to the protection of the building.

Policy

English policy on determining applications: the National Planning Policy Framework

The National Planning Policy Framework ("NPPF") sets out the Government's planning policies for England and how these should be applied.[260] These are relevant to the determination of planning applications and listed building consent applications. The current version of the NPPF was published in July 2021.

---

[257] The provisions are the planning Acts (meaning the Town and Country Planning Act 1990, the Planning (Listed Buildings and Conservation Areas) Act 1990, the Planning (Hazardous Substances) Act 1990 and the Planning (Consequential Provisions) Act 1990), Part I of the Historic Buildings and Ancient Monuments Act 1953 and sections 70 and 73 of the Leasehold Reform, Housing and Urban Development Act 1993: see the Planning (Listed Buildings and Conservation Areas) Act 1990, s. 72(2).

[258] *East Northamptonshire District Council v Secretary of State for Communities and Local Government* [2014] EWCA Civ 137, [2014] P&CR 22.

[259] Planning Act (Northern Ireland) 2011, s. 104(10).

[260] NPPF, § 1.

The NPPF describes heritage assets as "*an irreplaceable resource [which] should be conserved in a manner appropriate to their significance, so that they can be enjoyed for their contribution to the quality of life of existing and future generations*".[261] The two key concepts for present purposes in the NPPF are 'heritage assets' and 'designated heritage assets':[262]

a. Heritage asset is defined as "A building, monument, site, place, area or landscape identified as having a degree of significance meriting consideration in planning decisions, because of its heritage interest. It includes designated heritage assets and assets identified by the local planning authority (including local listing)".

b. Designated heritage asset is defined as "A World Heritage Site, Scheduled Monument, Listed Building, Protected Wreck Site, Registered Park and Garden, Registered Battlefield or Conservation Area designated under the relevant legislation".

An item which is a listed building in its own right would be a designated heritage asset. Similarly one which was part of a scheduled monument or listed building would be part of a designated heritage asset. An unlisted item may be a non-designated heritage asset.

The NPPF's chapter on conserving and enhancing the historic environment contains guidance on the approach to determining applications affecting heritage assets. It requires great weight to be given to the conservation of a designated heritage asset, as set out in paragraph 199:

> "*When considering the impact of a proposed development on the significance of a designated heritage asset, great weight should be given to the asset's conservation (and the more important the asset, the greater the weight should be). This is irrespective of whether any potential harm amounts to substantial harm, total loss or less than substantial harm to its significance.*"

---

261 NPPF, §189.

262 NPPF, Annex 2: Glossary.

By paragraph 200, a 'clear and convincing justification' must be given for any harm to such an asset:

> *"Any harm to, or loss of, the significance of a designated heritage asset (from its alteration or destruction, or from development within its setting), should require clear and convincing justification."*

Harm to designated heritage assets falls into one of two categories, substantial harm (which includes total loss) or less than substantial harm. The approach in cases of substantial harm is set out at paragraphs 200 and 201. Paragraph 200 addresses the approach where the asset is a grade II, II* or I listed building:

> *"200 ... Substantial harm to or loss of:*
>
> *a) grade II listed buildings, or grade II registered parks or gardens, should be exceptional;*
>
> *b) assets of the highest significance, notably scheduled monuments, protected wreck sites, registered battlefields, grade I and II* listed buildings, grade I and II* registered parks and gardens, and World Heritage Sites, should be wholly exceptional.*

For all other designated assets, where a proposed development will lead to substantial harm to (or total loss of significance of) the asset, consent should be refused, unless the substantial harm or total loss is necessary to achieve substantial public benefits that outweigh that harm or loss (or other, presently irrelevant, criteria apply). This is set out in paragraph 201:

> *Where a proposed development will lead to substantial harm to (or total loss of significance of) a designated heritage asset, local planning authorities should refuse consent, unless it can be demonstrated that the substantial harm or total loss is necessary to achieve substantial public benefits that outweigh that harm or loss, or all of the following apply:*
>
> *a) the nature of the heritage asset prevents all reasonable uses of the site; and*

> *b) no viable use of the heritage asset itself can be found in the medium term through appropriate marketing that will enable its conservation; and*
>
> *c) conservation by grant-funding or some form of not for profit, charitable or public ownership is demonstrably not possible; and*
>
> *d) the harm or loss is outweighed by the benefit of bringing the site back into use."*

Where less than substantial harm would be caused, "harm should be weighed against the public benefits of the proposal including, where appropriate, securing its optimum viable use". This is addressed at paragraph 202:

> *"Where a development proposal will lead to less than substantial harm to the significance of a designated heritage asset, this harm should be weighed against the public benefits of the proposal including, where appropriate, securing its optimum viable use."*

The approach where applications may impact heritage assets which are not designated is set out in paragraph 203:

> *"The effect of an application on the significance of a non-designated heritage asset should be taken into account in determining the application. In weighing applications that directly or indirectly affect non-designated heritage assets, a balanced judgement will be required having regard to the scale of any harm or loss and the significance of the heritage asset."*

An approach of 'retain and explain' for contested heritage was introduced in English planning policy by a Written Ministerial Statement on 18th January 2021.[263] The 'retain and explain' policy had previously been articulated in a letter from the Secretary of State for Digital, Culture, Media and Sport to various national museums and galleries and other arm's length bodies.[264] That emphasised that "*the Government does not*

---

263 Planning and Heritage Update by Robert Jenrick MP, UIN HCWS 713.

264 22nd September 2020.

support the removal of statues or other similar objects". That was then followed up in a Parliamentary debate on 25 September 2020. The January 2021 statement adopted the 25 September explanation by the Minister for Infrastructure as part of planning policy.

Subsequently the NPPF was revised, with effect from July 2021. The revised guidance contains new guidance specifically affecting historic statues, plaques, memorials or monuments. It leans towards retaining historic statues, plaques, memorials or monuments in situ and explaining their context, rather than removing them, but does not prohibit their removal. In a written ministerial statement made on 20 July 2021 to accompany the launch of the revised NPPF,[265]https://questions-statements.parliament.uk/written-statements/detail/2021-07-20/hcws216 the then Secretary of State for the Ministry of Housing, Communities and Local Government (Robert Jenrick) said that one of the policy changes in the NPPF was an "*emphasis of the importance of retaining and explaining the historic and social context of historic statues, plaques, memorials or monuments rather than removing them*".

Paragraph 195 of the NPPF advises:

> *"Local planning authorities should identify and assess the particular significance of any heritage asset that may be affected by a proposal (including by development affecting the setting of a heritage asset) taking account of the available evidence and any necessary expertise. They should take this into account when considering the impact of a proposal on a heritage asset, to avoid or minimise any conflict between the heritage asset's conservation and any aspect of the proposal."*

A new paragraph 198 emphasises the importance of retention of historic statues, plaques, memorials or monuments:

> "*In considering any applications to remove or alter a historic statue, plaque, memorial or monument (whether listed or not), local planning authorities should have regard to the importance of their retention in*

[265] Building Beautiful Places, statement UIN HCWS216, made on 20 July 2021.

> *situ and, where appropriate, of explaining their historic and social context rather than removal.*"

There has not yet been any appeal decision or court case considering the application of the new guidance on relocation of historic statutes or other memorials. It is should be noted that this part of the guidance does not establish a presumption in favour of their retention in *situ*. Rather, the guidance is to have regard to the importance of retention in *situ*. Where the item is listed it necessarily has significance. A historic quality to the item will indicate significance although that might not always be the case. The obligation to have regard to a matter means that it must be specifically considered.[266] The preference to 'retain and explain' rather than remove is clear in the policy. A preliminary point is whether any explanation is required, particularly if that looks like an excuse or apology, and that can be followed by a debate about what any explanation should be.

Welsh policy on determining applications

Planning Policy Wales ("PPW")[267] provides the national planning policy framework for the consideration of the historic environment. This is supplemented by guidance contained in Technical Advice Note 24: The Historic Environment and Cadw associated best practice guidance on the historic environment.

The general approach to the historic environment is set out at PPW paragraph 6.19:

> *"Any decisions made through the planning system must fully consider the impact on the historic environment and on the significance and heritage values of individual historic assets and their contribution to the character of place."*

[266] *Howell v Secretary of State for Communities and Local Government* [2014] EWHC 3627 (Admin) per Cranston J at §46.

[267] Edition 11, February 2021.

The guidance on listed building applications is at paragraphs 6.1.10 to 6.1.13. Paragraph 6.1.10 states:

> *"There should be a general presumption in favour of the preservation or enhancement of a listed building and its setting, which might extend beyond its curtilage. For any development proposal affecting a listed building or its setting, the primary material consideration is the statutory requirement to have special regard to the desirability of preserving the building, its setting or any features of special architectural or historic interest which it possesses."*

Paragraph 6.1.12 provides that "*the demolition of any listed building should be considered as exceptional and require the strongest justification*". Applicants for listed building consent must be able to justify why alteration or demolition is desirable or necessary and consider the impact of any chance upon its special architectural or historic interest.

Conservation area consent policy is in paragraphs 6.1.14 to 6.1.17. Paragraph 6.1.14 states that "*There should be a general presumption in favour of the preservation or enhancement of the character or appearance of conservation areas or their settings*". Paragraph 6.1.15 advises that "*there is a strong presumption against the granting of planning permission for developments... which damage the character or appearance of a conservation area or its setting to an unacceptable level*" and that "*In exceptional cases, the presumption may be overridden in favour of development considered desirable on public interest grounds*".

Northern Ireland policy on heritage matters in planning

Regional level planning policy in Northern Ireland on heritage matters is contained in the *Strategic Planning Policy Statement for Northern Ireland (SPPS) Planning for Sustainable Development*[268] and, until a plan strategy is adopted for the relevant local authority area, *Planning Policy Statement 6 (PPS 6) Planning, Archaeology and the Built Heritage.*[269] Archaeology

[268] Published by the Department of the Environment, September 2015.

[269] Department of the Environment, March 1999.

and built heritage is addressed in s. 6 of the SPPS. For listed buildings the SPPS says:[270]

> *"It is important that such development respects the essential character and architectural or historic interest of the building and its setting, and that features of special interest remain intact and unimpaired."*

Additionally:[271]

> *"Proposals for the total demolition of a listed building or any significant part of it must not be permitted unless there are exceptional reasons why it cannot be retained in its original or a reasonably modified form."*

In PPS6 policy BH6 takes a similar approach to the SPPS to listed buildings emphasising the use of traditional and sympathetic materials and the retention of architectural detailing. Exceptional circumstances are required for demolition by policy BH10.

Relevant and material considerations

As with all decisions taken by public bodies, decisions whether to grant regulatory consent must take into account relevant considerations whilst disregarding irrelevant considerations. For determining planning applications, the legislation refers to material considerations. They are approached in the same way, as matters material or relevant to the exercise of the particular power in its statutory context and for the purposes for which it was granted.[272]

Planning applications

What constitutes a material consideration in the determination of a planning application has received considerable attention. This is, in part,

---

[270] SPPS, § 6.13.

[271] SPPS, § 6.15.

[272] *R(Health and Safety Executive) v Wolverhampton City Council* [2012] UKSC 34, [2012] 1 W.L.R. 2264 at § 9 per Lord[272] Carnwath JSC.

because the statutory planning framework includes express requirements to have regard to material considerations, in addition to the general obligation that applies to decisions by public body decision makers. Section 70(2) of the TCPA requires a planning authority to have regard to the development plan and certain other matters "*so far as material to the application*" and to "*any other material considerations*": that is to say, material to the scheme which is proposed. Similarly, in relation to an application for planning permission, the "*material considerations*" referred to in the presumption in favour of the development plan in section 38(6) of the Planning and Compulsory Purchase Act 2004 are considerations material to the proposal.

To be a material consideration, the same legal tests apply as for the imposition of a planning condition:[273]

> *"the conditions imposed must be for a planning purpose and not for any ulterior one, and ... they must fairly and reasonably relate to the development permitted. Also they must not be so unreasonable that no reasonable planning authority could have imposed them ..."*

A planning purpose is one which relates to the character of the use of land.[274]

Relevant or material considerations are split between those which the decision maker is obliged to take into account and those which the decision maker may choose to take into account:[275]

(i) Considerations which have to be taken into account may be expressly required by statute,[276] implicitly required by the

---

[273] *Newbury District Council v Secretary of State for the Environment* [1981] AC 578 at 599-600 per Viscount Dilhorne, applied to material considerations most recently in *Wright* at §32, 34 per Lord Sales JSC.

[274] *Westminster City Council v Great Portland Estates Plc* [1985] AC 661 at p.670 per Lord Scarman.

[275] See *R (Friends of the Earth Limited) v Secretary of State for Transport* [2020] UKSC 52, [2021] PTSR 190 at §116-121.

[276] Such as regard to effects on listed buildings and conservation areas: Planning (Listed Buildings and Conservation Areas) Act 1990, ss. 16, 66, 72.

statue, explicitly (or possibly implicitly) required to be considered by a policy[277] (which must itself need to be considered[278]), or , a matter which is so *"obviously material"*, that it is irrational not to take it into account.

(ii) Other relevant or material considerations which the decision maker may take into account, but would not be acting unlawfully if it did not do so.

In the context of contested heritage cases it is worth considering to what extent the effect of an object on a person's feelings might be legitimately considered. Land use might have effects on behaviour which are relevant in planning terms. In *Finlay v Secretary of State for the Environment*[279] the Secretary of State was entitled to consider that one factor for refusing planning permission for a private members club where sexually explicit films were to be shown was that it shared an entrance with a maisonette and was likely to discourage, and could effectively prevent, the occupation of the residential accommodation. Forbes J held that the Secretary of State was not saying "I dislike pornographic films" what he was saying was a pure planning matter, namely if people show pornographic films downstairs, it was likely to be a deterrent to potential occupiers of the residential accommodation upstairs. The Minister was also entitled to say "*the showing of sexually explicit films may be expected in most circumstances to have the effect of altering the environmental character of an area by introducing a type of use which is detrimental to the amenities of neighbouring residential property, and also to some commercial uses, because many people would find this type of use objectionable, and consequently, avoid the area*". The judge observed that "*the Secretary of State is there expressing in relation to the type of film being shown is not, as it were, a moral judgment on the films themselves or their nature or character, it is merely a planning judgment on the question of whether the exhibition of*

[277] See *R(Save Stonehenge World Heritage Site Ltd) v Secretary of State for Transport* [2021] EWHC 2161 (Admin), [2022] P.T.S.R. 74 at § 61 per Holgate J. Such as the tests for decisions affecting heritage assets in national planning policy.

[278] In this context national planning policy, such as the NPPF, PPW or SPPS is obviously material and has to be considered.

[279] [1982] JPL 802.

films of that kind is going to have a planning impact on the area". A person's feelings passing a particular site may be relevant. In *Lewstar Ltd v Secretary of State for the Environment*[280] an Inspector refused planning permission for a peep show in a narrow pedestrian way which already contained sex-related businesses. The Inspector was entitled to conclude that approving a further business would have an adverse effect on the character of the area, the way's functioning as an important pedestrian link and upon the amenity of residents having found that 'to traverse this Court can be an unpleasant, embarrassing and even intimidating experience for a reasonable and tolerant person'.

In both cases there was a distinction between a dislike (or even personal opposition or revulsion) about the use, which is not relevant, and that personal opinion causing an alteration in activity in the vicinity. If the use discouraged people from occupying the upstairs flat or walking down an alleyway then that was a landuse effect which could be relevant. In the context of an alleged offensive statue or monument, there would need to be sufficient evidence that it discouraged people from going to a particular location for it to be potentially relevant.

In *R (Copeland) v London Borough of Tower Hamlets*[281] the proximity of a proposed fast food take-away to a school, and so its effect on healthy eating by schoolchildren, was capable of being material.[282] That finding related to the physical relationship between the two uses. Cranston J said more generally:[283]

> *"Promoting social objectives may be a material consideration in the planning context. Planning controls in order to promote social objectives are considerations which can relate to physical land use. Whether a social objective is relevant in a particular case turns on the circumstances. As long as the promotion of the social goal is lawfully*

280 [1984] JPL 116.

281 [2010] EWHC 1845 (Admin), [2011] JPL 40.

282 Approved in *Wright* at § 51 per Lord Sales JSC.

283 At § 22.

> *within the planning sphere it matters not that it falls elsewhere as well."*

In *West Midlands Probation Committee v Secretary of State for the Environment* [284] the fears of local residents that crime and anti-social behaviour would be caused by the expansion of a bail hostel was capable of being a material consideration.

R (Wright) v Forest of Dean Council ("*Wright*")[285] concerned a community fund being offered by a wind turbine developer, similar funds having been used elsewhere to provide a defibrillator for the village halls, a village handyman service, installation of heaters in a church, repairs to almshouses, waterproof clothing for children at a playgroup and a meal at local pub for lunch club volunteers. The Supreme Court agreed with the High Court and the Court of Appeal that the community fund was immaterial to the determination of the planning application and so the planning permission was unlawfully granted. Lord Sales said:[286]

> *"The benefits were not proposed as a means of pursuing any proper planning purpose, but for the ulterior purpose of providing general benefits to the community. Moreover, they did not fairly and reasonably relate to the development for which permission was sought. ... The community benefits to be provided by Resilient Severndale did not affect the use of the land. Instead, they were proffered as a general inducement to the Council to grant planning permission and constituted a method of seeking to buy the permission sought, in breach of the principle that planning permission cannot be bought or sold."*

To be material, a benefit must have a connection with the use or the presence of development on the land which is the subject of the application. Issues in earlier cases were not based on opposition to the sex or fast food industries in general, but the effects of the particular proposal in the particular location. In *Wright* (as in the financial benefits cases it

---

284 (1998) 76 P & CR 589.

285 [2016] EWHC 1349 (Admin), [2016] JPL 1235 at §20 per Dove J.

286 *Wright* (Supreme Court) at §44.

refers to) there was a need for the spending of the benefit to be related to the development permitted. In the context of contested heritage such considerations must relate to the effects of the particular item in the particular location.

Listed building consent applications

The only matters specifically identified in determining listed building consent applications are giving special regard to the desirability of preserving the listed building, its setting or any features of special architectural or historic interest which it possesses[287] and the special attention to preserving or enhancing the character and appearance of any conservation area that the listed building is in.[288] The relevance of other considerations to a listed building consent application has received little attention. They must, though, relate to the application, so to the presence, condition, setting or significance of the listed building.

Land use planning effects, such as those in the 'discouragement' cases above, may be relevant to the existence of public benefits which may justify harm.

Public Sector Equality Duty

In England and Wales[289], a planning authority determining a listed building or planning application,[290] and the Secretary of State

---

[287] Listed Buildings Act, s. 16(2).

[288] Listed Buildings Act, s. 72.

[289] The Equality Act 2010 does not apply in Northern Ireland. A statutory duty on public authorities to have regard to the need to promote equality of opportunity between persons of different religious belief, political opinion, racial group, age, marital status or sexual orientation, between men and women, and between persons with a disability and persons without is contained in s.75 of the Northern Ireland Act 1998. Section 75(2) also requires that a public authority in carrying out its functions relating to Northern Ireland shall have regard to the desirability of promoting good relations between persons of different religious belief, political opinion or racial group.

[290] *R(Buckley) v Bath and North East Somerset Council* [2018] EWHC 1551 (Admin), [2019] PTSR 335.

determining an application for scheduled monument consent, must, as public authorities exercising public functions, comply with the Public Sector Equality Duty (PSED) in s. 149(1) of the Equality Act 2010:

> *"A public authority must, in the exercise of its functions, have due regard to the need to—*
>
> *(a) eliminate discrimination, harassment, victimisation and any other conduct that is prohibited by or under this Act;*
>
> *(b) advance equality of opportunity between persons who share a relevant protected characteristic and persons who do not share it;*
>
> *(c) foster good relations between persons who share a relevant protected characteristic and persons who do not share it."*

The relevant protected characteristics are age, disability, gender reassignment, pregnancy and maternity, race, religion or belief, sex and sexual orientation.[291] These matters are explained, in part, further in s. 149:

> *"(3) Having due regard to the need to advance equality of opportunity between persons who share a relevant protected characteristic and persons who do not share it involves having due regard, in particular, to the need to—*
>
> *(a) remove or minimise disadvantages suffered by persons who share a relevant protected characteristic that are connected to that characteristic;*
>
> *(b) take steps to meet the needs of persons who share a relevant protected characteristic that are different from the needs of persons who do not share it;*

[291] Equality Act 2010, s. 149(7).

(c) encourage persons who share a relevant protected characteristic to participate in public life or in any other activity in which participation by such persons is disproportionately low.

...

(5) Having due regard to the need to foster good relations between persons who share a relevant protected characteristic and persons who do not share it involves having due regard, in particular, to the need to—

(a) tackle prejudice, and

(b) promote understanding.

(6) Compliance with the duties in this section may involve treating some persons more favourably than others; but that is not to be taken as permitting conduct that would otherwise be prohibited by or under this Act."

To support the general duty, the Equality Act 2010 allows for the enactment of specific duties. The specific duties are devolved powers, and this has resulted in different specific duties being set in Wales and England. In England, the Equality Act 2010 (Specific Duties) Regulations 2011 require public authorities to publish equality objectives and information to demonstrate compliance with the general equality duty. In Wales, the PSED goes further and contains express provisions about engagement (Regulation 5) and equality impact assessments (Regulation 8) which are not present in the English PSED.

Regulatory consents and the removal of works of art

In preparing and considering an application for the removal of a heritage asset the first question is whether the removal would cause harm. That depends on the importance of the asset in context: for example the removal of a statue which is part of a listed building and contributes to its significance is more likely to be harmful than a removing a work which has been recently attached to a new building, without having been required by any planning condition.

That requires an assessment of the object, its history in the location and, in particular, the interest attaching to any building or site it is part of. If harm arises (or might be seen to arise), the issues are then how to minimise the harm and then to justify any residual harm.

In respect of minimisation of the harm, a question may be whether and how the item is to be replaced. A replacement (of perhaps lower value) would avoid a gap and could in some circumstances be seen as a better fit. There may be potential benefits from where the item is to be moved to or conceivably the use to be made of proceeds of sale.

An application might therefore be made for the removal of the item to a particular location, or seeking to conditions which govern its future siting, or simply allowing for the removal of the item. In the latter case what then happens to it is a matter for the owner.

A pre-NPPF example was the grant of listed building consent on appeal for the replacement of a gilt-wood chandelier with an 18th century brass chandelier at The Chapel, Sir William Turner's Court, Kirkleatham.[292] A baroque chandelier had been hanging in the late 17th and mid 18th Century, Grade I listed chapel at the Kirkleatham almshouse since about 1747 when had been acquired in a sale. The appeal inspector considered that because of a clash of designs, its removal would not be harmful:

> "*8. … The chandelier is visually heavy and, in its gilt wood construction, relatively solid in appearance. It interrupts views across the building, including detracting from the fine stained glass window in the east end. Proportionally and visually it appears out of kilter with the galleried space around it. That is in no small measure due to its ornate Baroque style compared with the predominant simplicity of the chapel's Palladium architecture.*
>
> *9. It does not, I consider, play a pivotal or intrinsic role in the design of what is a small scaled interior. It loss would not therefore harm its*

292 Inspector's appeal decision 20 August 2007, ref: APP/V0728/E/07/2040520.

preservation, although crucially the interior space would be less complete without a replacement of an appropriate design."

A Dutch, 20 light, brass chandelier of a design and age contemporary with the mid 18th century remodelling of the chapel was an appropriate replacement. The Inspector also gave some weight to financial benefits to the repair of the chapel and serving the associated almshouses.

Regulatory consent and contested heritage

This final section considers how issues relating to contested heritage assets may be relevant to the determination of applications for regulatory consent for the removal or alteration of a heritage asset.

The NPPF's approach, that planning authorities should have "*regard to the importance of their retention in situ and, where appropriate, of explaining their historic and social context rather than removal*",[293] emphasises a priority to the retention of the historic environment. Concerns about who or what is represented is sought to be addressed by explanation rather than refusal.

Prior to the amendment to the NPPF, but consistent with it, Historic England has produced guidance in the form of a checklist to help local planning authorities to identify and assess relevant considerations in contested heritage cases. This guidance is summarised below, before consideration is given to how contested heritage issues may arise in relation to the following:

(1) In relation to heritage assets which are listed buildings, whether contested heritage concerns could be relevant to the special architectural or historic interest of the asset.

(2) In relation to heritage assets located in conservation areas, whether contested heritage concerns could be relevant to

[293] NPPF, § 198.

assessing the impact of proposed works on the character or appearance of a conservation areas.

(3) In relation to heritage assets which are "designated heritage assets" whether contested heritage concerns are relevant to assessing the level of harm caused by its removal or alteration, or the public benefit which would result from its removal or alteration, for the purposes of applying the harm test in the NPPF.

(4) In relation to all heritage assets, whether contested heritage concerns are relevant to a public body decision-maker's discharge of their public sector equalities duty.

Historic England's checklist for contested heritage decisions

The introduction to the checklist acknowledges the complexity raised by applications relating to contested heritage:

> *"Historic England is acutely aware that certain representations of history in our public realm today can cause offence. The statues, monuments and other commemorative structures that society keeps and protects – for a number of reasons – do not always represent contemporary values, and some are distinctly at odds with them. In such situations there are sometimes calls to remove or alter the statue or monument, and this may precipitate planning and/or listed building consent applications. It is important to recognise that as a group they represent our collective past and as such have a significant heritage value."*

It goes on to explain that Historic England's stance on historic statues and sites which have become contested is to retain and explain them. It acknowledges, however, that the decision-making body is usually the local planning authority and sets out guidance designed to enable those authorities to make a balanced decision. The checklist identifies the following questions to consider:

1. *Are there any particularly contested or challenging assets in the local authority area for which it would be worth facilitating discussions, and/or inviting applications for their contextualisation?*

2. *Does the authority have enough information about the heritage asset in question, from an appropriate range of sources, to understand its significance?* 'Significance,' in this context, is defined as 'the value of a heritage asset to this and future generations because of its historic interest,' which may be 'archaeological, architectural, artistic or historic.' The checklist adds that 'Understanding what is significant about a historic object or site includes all the diverse values or interests that people associate with it. Eliciting and understanding community perspectives will be important within this process…. It will [also] include the reasons for its creation, and why it is being challenged now.'

3. *Does the authority have enough information about any proposed changes to be able to understand the impact on the heritage asset (or assets) and make a decision in accordance with the NPPF* (the National Planning Policy Framework)*?*

4. *If the proposals damage what is important about the heritage asset, or the contribution that the setting makes to other assets, what is the nature of that impact?* The checklist notes that impacts might be direct physical ones, or indirect ones and, very occasionally, impacts brought about by a change of use without any physical change. The impact on the contribution to settings of heritage assets in the wider area will also need to be considered.

5. *Assuming that the proposed alternations and changes cause some damage to the heritage asset, is that damage necessary?*

6. *Is there sufficient justification for the proposed level of damage caused?* The checklist states that on contested sites the authority may need to plan for a greater volume of information provided by third parties and demonstrate how this has been taken into account when the authority makes a decision.'

7. *When dealing with designated heritage assets, what are the public benefits of the proposal?*

8. *The balancing act: where necessary and justified, is the damage outweighed by the public benefit?*

Relevance of contested heritage concerns to special architectural or historic interest of the heritage asset for the purposes of applications to relocate, remove or de-list a listed building

As noted above, local planning authorities or the Secretary of State are required by the Listed Buildings Act 1990 to have special regard to the desirability of preserving a listed building building's special architectural or historic interest when deciding whether to grant planning permission or listed building consent, or whether to de-list a building. The question which may arise is whether the association of the heritage asset with historical iniquities, or concerns about the character, opinions or conduct of the person memorialised, affects its special architectural or historic interest.

The starting point is to identify the special architectural or historic interest of the listed building in question. This may be recorded in the building's list entry, although the amount of information provided in the listing varies considerably. The initial decision that a building has special architectural or historic interest is a matter of judgement for the Secretary of State at the time of listing, to be taken following consultation with English Heritage and any other expert he considers appropriate.[294] The Department for Digital, Culture, Media & Sport has published '*Principles of Selection for Listed Buildings*' which operate as guidance in England on the approach that the Secretary of State will take to listing decisions.[295] The guidance states "*To be able to justify special historic interest a building must illustrate important aspects of the nation's history*

[294] Listed Buildings Act 1990, s. 1(4).

[295] The Northern Ireland Department for Communities Historic Environment Division has published *Criteria for the Scheduling of Historic Monuments and the Listing of Buildings of Special Architectural or Historic Interest, with associated procedures* (May 2019).

and / or have closely substantiated historical associations with nationally important individuals, groups or events".[296]

As a factor also relevant to heritage assets, architectural interest may include artistic interest and aesthetic merits.[297] The Historic England Listing Selection Guides provide more assistance on particular types of buildings. Of particular relevance to cases raising contested heritage issues is the '*Commemorative Structures Listing Selection Guide*'. This includes public and civic monuments as well as funerary monuments. The Guide notes the significance which these can have in public space:

> *"The early years of the eighteenth century witnessed a rise in the erection of public statues and monuments. Often the work of the leading architects and sculptors of their day, they form the visual centrepiece of formal architectural compositions and public spaces, and are thus very prominent indeed."*[298]

On public statuary the guide notes:

> *"Statues and sculptures are often prominent features within the public realm and private grounds alike, and are often of high aesthetic quality and historic interest. These generally will have been identified and should normally be protected."*[299]

Victorian public sculpture is noted as often possessing "*considerable sculptural merit and will generally always warrant designation, and sometimes at a high grade*". On the identity of individuals the guidance says on tombstones:

> *"Historic interest of the individual commemorated will often be attached to tombs of famous people, as is the case with monuments of an earlier date and may be supported by special architectural or sculptural quality, or by striking epitaphs. Again, inclusion in the*

---

[296] *Principles of Selection for Listed Buildings*, § 16.

[297] *Principles of Selection for Listed Buildings*, §§ 16, 19.

[298] *Commemorative Structures Listing Selection Guide*, p. 3.

[299] *Commemorative Structures Listing Selection Guide*, p. 12.

> *Oxford Dictionary of National Biography is a useful yard-stick to check the level of interest against. Candidates will need to be judged on a case-by-case basis: in all cases, the aim is to identify tombs of persons of national interest.*"[300]

The guidance states that a commemorative structure may be of historic interest as a source of information about past lives and the evolution of English society, giving as examples the tombstones of former slaves[301] or early members of distinct faith groups. Key factors in listing will tend to be the architectural, including artistic, qualities of the statue and its relationship with its location. The identity of the individual commemorated will be of less importance, unless they are a figure of some national note, in which case the statue is likely to be of high quality in any event.

Whether or not contemporary concerns about the association of a listed building with historical iniquities, or concern about the character, opinions or conduct of the person memorialised, affect the special architectural or historic interest is clearly a fact-sensitive question. However, the following general observations can be made having regard to the statutory criteria and the listing guidance.

- A heritage asset commemorating an individual or event may be listed in whole or in part for its architectural interest as opposed to its historic interest. For example, one the reasons given for the designation of the now world-famous statue of Edward Colston, located in Bristol centre until its removal, was its "*group value with other Bristol memorials: a statute of Edmund Burke, the Cenotaph, and a drinking fountain commemorating the Industrial and Fine Art Exhibition of 1893*". It is difficult to see how concerns about the character of Colston and his

[300] *Commemorative Structures Listing Selection Guide*, p. 4.

[301] *Commemorative Structures Listing Selection Guide*, page 10. It gives the example of the headstone and foot stone of Scipio Africanus (d.1720), Henbury, Bristol, which is listed grade II* for its historic interest.

associations with the slave trade could affect the architectural interest of the statute.

- The historic interest of the person represented in a public statue may be part of the special interest. The list entry for the Edward Colston statue in Bristol is also pertinent here, including in the reasons for designation "*The statue is of particular historical interest, the subject being Edward Colston, Bristol's most famous philanthropist, now also noted for his involvement in the slave trade.*" So whether the person represented is of historic interest is relevant to special interest, and so to significance and the level of harm.[302] The importance of this in practice may be more limited. That an individual may have been objectionable in some way does not necessarily reduce the interest in them. The historic interest of a heritage asset will not necessarily derive from the actions of the person or event commemorated, still less from approval of the individual or event commemorated. A heritage asset memorialising an individual or event may be of historic interest on the basis that it illustrates an important aspect of a nation's history (to use the wording of '*Principles of Selection for Listed Buildings*') or provide a source of information about the evolution of English society (to use the wording of Historic England's '*Commemorative Structures Listing Selection Guide*'). The fact that some of the activities of individual commemorated may now be seen to be objectionable, such as involvement in slavery, would not necessarily affect this aspect of the historic interest of the heritage asset.

- A question may be whether the special architectural or historic interest of a heritage asset which has been designated as a listed building is linked to its location. Again, this is a question of

[302] In a listed building appeal decision for the temporary siting of a replacement statue on the Colston plinth, the Inspector found that special interest of the listed building was "*focussed partly on the design detailing of the Edward Colston statue and the plinth, and partly on the depiction of a citizen who has been remembered by some for his philanthropic acts in Bristol*": APP/Z0116/W/3260461 at § 16.

> fact that will depend on the reasons for designation and subsequent evaluations in particular cases. Most of the special architectural interest in a statue is likely to derive from the physical characteristics of the statue. It is unlikely to be listed otherwise, as distinct from potentially contributing to the special interest of a conservation area. Its setting may contribute to its interest and it may contribute to the interest of its surroundings: a public square can be enhanced by statues or public art. The subject goes to two potential issues: the harm caused by moving the item and whether the present location confers a degree of support for the figure represented (beyond the display of the work in the first place) which affects any public benefits in its removal or relocation...

Relevance of contested heritage concerns to the character or appearance of a conservation area

Where a building is located in a conservation area in England and Wales, there is a statutory requirement to pay special attention to the desirability of "*preserving or enhancing the character of that area*".

The NPPF includes conservation areas within designated heritage assets. The approach to demolition of unlisted buildings in conservation areas is set out at paragraph 207, which states:

> *"Not all elements of a Conservation Area or World Heritage Site will necessarily contribute to its significance. Loss of a building (or other element) which makes a positive contribution to the significance of the Conservation Area or World Heritage Site should be treated either as substantial harm under paragraph 201 or less than substantial harm under paragraph 202, as appropriate, taking into account the relative significance of the element affected and its contribution to the significance of the Conservation Area or World Heritage Site as a whole."*

Thus, it is only if a building makes a positive contribution to the significant of the conservation area that the herm tests in the NPPF are to be applied. In *Fulford v Secretary of State for the Environment*[303] (a case which concerned planning policy in PPG 15 preceding the NPPF), Stephen Richards, sitting as a Deputy High Court judge, held that "*positive contribution*" was to be given it ordinary meaning, with the qualification that a certain degree of positive contribution was required as it must be something more than little.

Determining whether a building makes a "*positive contribution*" to a conservation area, and whether its removal would "*preserve or enhance the character of the area*" may require consideration of the interaction between building and its context. It may be said that where the continued presence of a heritage asset in a particular location causes offence due to the types of contested heritage concerns raised above, its removal would enhance the character of the area. Likewise, it might be said that in such circumstances a heritage asset does not make a positive contribution to the area.

Relevance of contested heritage concerns to the application of the harm test in the NPPF, or as a material consideration

Contested heritage concerns may be relevant to determining harm to the designated heritage asset or public benefits.

A variety of factors will affect the harm which would be caused by the removal or alteration of a heritage asset which is a listed building. These will include whether the item is to be destroyed, and if retained whether there are proposals for its reinstatement, and what is proposed for the site. Where that context in which it is placed contributes to the item's significance, harm would undoubtedly result from its removal. The scale of that has, though, to be affected by the survival of the item and, to a degree, where it ends up. These will have different bearings on the elements which make up the significance of the listed building.[304] The relevance of these matters derives from the statutory test of special architectural and historic interest in the designation of a listed building

[303] Unreported, 26 March 1997.

[304] Significance would be assessed with regard to *Managing Significance in Decision-Taking in the Historic Environment Historic Environment Good Practice Advice in Planning: 2.*

and the duty to have special regard to its preservation. As discussed above, contested heritage concerns may be relevant to the current special architectural and historic interest in the designation of a heritage asset.

The present-day reaction to character and actions of the individual memorialised might be relevant to whether there are public benefits from the removal of a heritage asset. For example, if the presence of a statue or memorial in a particular location has caused upset because of the conduct of the person memorialised, and this has resulted in a land use effect, then removal is capable of being a public benefit which might be seen to outweigh the harm to the historic environment of removing the statue.[305]

Outside of the context of the NPPF, contested heritage concerns may be relevant or material considerations which can be taken into account when determining a listed building or planning application. However, as explained above, a matter can only be taken into account when determining a listed building or planning application if it is a relevant or material consideration. It must concern a land use or listed building purpose and fairly and reasonably relate to the application. The sex establishment, bail hostel and fast food cases all concerned the land use effects of the particular premises: discouraging pedestrians or residential use of premises, local fear of crime, or children buying fried chicken after school. It is local effect which may be relevant, such as on the character of a particular square, possibly its city or an institution. Those effects must go beyond a general disapproval of the person or the statue and to some degree of impact or discouragement: for example, making the square or institution a distinctly less attractive place to be.

Equalities considerations

In the case of an application for removal or alteration of a contested heritage asset, regard should be had to the impacts of both granting and refusing the application on furthering the equality objectives. In the case of contested heritage, where communities are divided as to the appropriate response to memorials and statues of historical figures, both

[305] The issue of Confederate statues in the USA is discussed in Remembering to Forget: Correcting the False History of the Lost Cause in the American South through *Damnatio Memoriae* (Alicia Dixon) (2020) Vol XXV *Art Antiquity and Law* 189.

decisions granting and refusing permission to remove or alter the asset in question can have impacts relevant to the equality aims. For example, the presence of a statue might discourage persons with particular protected characteristics from using a public space associated with that statue. A decision to remove the statue might further the aim of encouraging persons who share a relevant protected characteristic to participate in public life. It might also advance equality of opportunity between persons who share a relevant protected characteristic with those who do not and foster good relations between different communities. However, the removal of a particular statute might cause disquiet amongst people with a different protected characteristics. Good relations between different communities might be undermined, rather than enhanced, by removal.

The diversity of opinions which can be generated by proposals to remove or alter contested heritage is well illustrated by the Report of a Commission of Inquiry established by Oriel College into issues associated with memorials to Cecil Rhodes.[306] The Commission was established by the Governing Body of Oriel College, Oxford, following public protests and wider debate about the College's memorials to Cecil Rhodes. The Governing Body expressed their wish to remove two memorials to Rhodes: a statue of Rhodes on the High Street Building, which has an associated inscription expressing gratitude for Rhodes' benefaction; and a plaque with a head and shoulders portrait of Rhodes and an inscription praising his '*great services rendered … to his country*,' located on the wall of a building owned by the College. The Report noted that there was a high degree of polarisation between those who would remove and those who would retain the memorials.[307]

It is therefore key in all cases that steps are taken to obtain different perspectives on the proposed course of action.

---

[306] April 2021, available online.

[307] Report, § 5.63.

CHAPTER FIVE

STREET NAMES

One way of celebrating or memorialising an individual has been to name a street after them. Indeed, one way of identifying when a street was laid out is to see who it was named after. Some of those names may become contentious over time. Various contested heritage arguments have arisen over street names: for example, Sir John Hawkins Square in Plymouth was renamed from the Elizabethan naval commander and early slave trader, to that of Jack Leslie, who was the only black professional footballer in England in the 1920s.

Street-naming powers

Outside Greater London the available street-renaming powers are the Public Health Acts Amendment Act 1907, s. 21 ("the 1907 Act") and the Public Health Act 1925, s. 18 ("the 1925 Act"). Which provisions apply depends initially on which were applicable prior to 1974[308] . The Public Health Act 1925 had allowed urban authorities (but not rural district councils) to adopt its provisions, but did not require that to be done/[309]. Subsequently a local authority may resolve to apply one provision or another, having given prior public notice.[310]. Only one power is available to a local authority at any time. There is no national register of which power applies and local authorities may have to search their records with care to determine what is applicable.

The Towns Improvement Clauses Act 1847, s. 64. authorises councils which had adopted its provisions to name streets.[311]. However s. 64

[308] Local Government Act 1972, Schedule 14, §§ 23, 24.

[309] Public Health Act 1925, s.3.

[310] Local Government Act 1972, Schedule 14, § 25.

[311] The Act contains standard clauses for local or private Acts

cannot be used to change the previously adopted name of a street.[312] In *Collins* the Lord Chief Justice, Lord Alverstone, observed that the Court 'can easily see that in the case of altering the name of an old street great inconvenience and difficulty may be caused if an alteration of name is forced upon people'.

The London Building Acts (Amendment) Act 1939, s. 6(1) authorise the borough council to name "*any street way place row of houses or block of buildings whether or not in substitution of for a name already given or assigned*". These powers originally applied to the London County Council area and were extended to the whole of Greater London by the London Government Act 1963, s. 43(1). The street-naming provisions of 1907 and 1925 Acts are disapplied in Greater London.[313]

None of the provisions sets out statutory criteria for street naming or identifies any matters that must be taken into account. The Secretary of State has not had any policy on street naming. Some guidance has been prepared at the local government level. GeoPlace LLP is a public sector limited liability partnership between the Local Government Association (LGA) and Ordnance Survey. It produces the 'GeoPlace Data Entry Conventions and Best Practice for Addresses'.[314] This is concerned principally with consistent data recording for mapping purposes (the working party which drew it up appears to be technical rather than political). It proposes that local authorities have policies for naming new streets, including the use of names of historic, deceased or living people.[315] However, other than discouraging the use of the names of living persons, the guidance provides no assistance on how this should be done.

The 1907 Act power may only be exercised with the consent of two-thirds of the non-domestic ratepayers and council tax payers in the

312 *Collins v Hornsey Urban Council* [1901] 2 KB 180 at p. 184 per Lord Alverstone CJ.

313 Local Government Act 1972, Schedule 14, § 26.

314 Presently version 3.4 (September 2016).

315 See § 4.2 with examples in Appendix F.

street.[316] The 1925 Act and the London Buildings Acts Amendment Act 1939 (s 6) are subject to no such requirement for consent. Consultation in advance of a naming decision (whether for a new street or a change of name) is required in the London legislation, but not under the 1925 Act. Street naming in Northern Ireland is governed by the Local Government (Miscellaneous Provisions) (Northern Ireland) Order 1995 which replaced the Towns Improvement Clauses Act 1847 and Public Health Acts Amendment Act 1907 provisions and other Northern Irish legislation.[317] Any street nameplate must express the name in English. The name may also be expressed in any other language on the nameplate or on a second nameplate.[318] In practice the other language would only be Irish. In deciding whether or not to display a second language nameplate, the "*council shall have regard to any views on the matter expressed by the occupiers of premises in that street*".[319]

The super-majority approach required by the 1907 Act may be introduced in local policy as a factor before the council would support a change. This arose in the related context of whether to erect dual-language street name plates in Northern Ireland. The High Court considered that a council policy to require the positive support of two-thirds of electors on the electoral register for the street before installing a second language name plate was lawful.[320]

A right to be consulted only arises if the legislation provides for it; a promise or practice of the decision maker gives rise to a legitimate

---

[316] The government has proposed replacing the various provisions in England with new legislation requiring a two-thirds majority of the local electorate for any street renaming, following the principles of the 1907 Act: see *Technical consultation on street naming* (11 April 2022).

[317] Local Government (Miscellaneous Provisions) (Northern Ireland) Order 1995, art 11(1)(a).

[318] Local Government (Miscellaneous Provisions) (Northern Ireland) Order 1995, art 11(1)(b), (2).

[319] Local Government (Miscellaneous Provisions) (Northern Ireland) Order 1995, art 11(4).

[320] *In the matter of an application by Eileen Reid for Judicial Review* [2014] NIQB 129.

expectation that it would be carried out; or fairness requires consultation to take place.

Appeals and challenges

There is a right of appeal under the 1925 Act to the magistrates' court: 1925 Act, s 8. An appeal is to be made by way of complaint.[321] Simply writing to the Court is at least formally defective: this may explain why only a small number of objections made to the Court appear to have been accepted as appeals in the Sir John Hawkins, Plymouth case. These are formal court proceedings, using the civil jurisdiction of the magistrates' court, which are old and poorly explained, so are not easy for the public to use.

The ability of the Court to differ from the council in an appeal is in practice very limited. In *Basildon Borough Council v James* ("*Basildon*")[322] the High Court held that an appeal under the 1925 Act can only be upheld if the court was satisfied that the council's decision was wrong.[323] It is not for the court to decide simply whether it would have altered the name. Nor conversely is the court limited to approaching the council decision on the basis of a public law error, as is done in judicial review. The High Court was consciously following the caselaw on appeals to the magistrates in alcohol licensing cases where the appellant "*should have to persuade the magistrates' court that the sub-committee should not have exercised its discretion in the way that it did rather than that the magistrates' court should be required to exercise a discretion afresh on the hearing of the appeal*".[324] The Court should though "*pay great attention to the opinion of the council as the duly constituted and elected local authority and should not lightly reverse its conclusion*".[325]

---

[321] Magistrates' Court Rules 1981, rule 34.

[322] [2015] EWHC 3365 (Admin), [2016] PTSR 377.

[323] *Basildon* at § 43 per Garnham J.

[324] *R(Hope & Glory Public House Ltd) v City of Westminster Magistrates' Court* [2011] EWCA Civ 31, [2011] PTSR 868.

[325] *Basildon* at § 43 per Garnham J.

It has to be remembered that licensing is subject to statutory licensing objectives, licensing policy which is adopted locally and derived from government policy, is regularly dealt with and subject to many comparable local decisions. Magistrates' courts can and do overturn local authority licensing decisions.

However, as the High Court pointed out in *Basildon* there *"are no statutory objectives, no statutory guidance and no policy to which the council was required to have regard or to which the court can have resort"* in changing street names.[326] This is the problem for anyone seeking to appeal a renaming decision. The Court has no criteria for deciding whether the council were wrong. Renaming is essentially an administrative decision, which may have political elements (particularly if the existing name is being considered unacceptable) and practical consequences. The court, whether lay magistrates or a professional district judge, are likely to be deferential to that administrative or political decision. In the absence of any statutory or policy tests which the council and the court should be applying or considering, it is very difficult for a judge to say that the council's view is wrong, even if the judge would have made a different decision for rational reasons themselves. In practice an appeal is more likely to succeed where there has effectively been a public law error, such as the council not following its own procedure or leaving out an obviously relevant issue, and so the court might then make up its own mind. It should also be noted that the *Basildon* case refers to the magistrates' court rejecting renaming proposals elsewhere in the town "*largely on technical grounds*"[327]) but it is not apparent on what basis this was done.

The alteration of a street-name under the 1907 Act appears to be subject to a right of appeal to the Crown Court under s. 7 of that Act by any person aggrieved, provided that to 'alter' a street name is included within a 'determination' or 'requirement' of the local authority which can be the subject of an appeal. If such an appeal right exists, it will be approached in the same way as in *Basildon*. There appears to be no right of appeal

[326] *Basildon* at § 36 per Garnham J.

[327] *Basildon* at § 5 per Garnham J.

against a decision under the London legislation, so a complainant's only remedy would be to apply to the High Court for judicial review.

CHAPTER SIX

THE CHURCH OF ENGLAND

The removal of artworks and other treasures from the Church of England's churches and other buildings are authorised by the grant of a faculty by the consistory courts and archdeacons. Listed buildings which are subject to the faculty jurisdiction are excused from listed building control by the ecclesiastical exemption.[328]

The faculty process is contained in the Ecclesiastical Jurisdiction and Care of Churches Measure 2018 No 3 and Faculty Jurisdiction Rules 2015.[329]

The faculty jurisdiction extends to every parish church, and churchyard and "article appertaining to it".[330] It therefore includes chattels of interest which are not fixtures or part of the building. It also includes buildings licensed for public worship and their articles unless otherwise ordered by the bishop of the diocese.[331] Where a building is exempted under these provisions, the bishop may order any particular article appertaining to the building to be subject to the jurisdiction by reason of its outstanding architectural, artistic, historical or archaeological value, significant monetary value or special risk of being stolen or damaged.[332]

Faculties are granted by the chancellor of the diocese. Some minor works or disposals may be carried out under a notice from the archdeacon but

---

[328] Planning (Listed Buildings and Conservation Areas) Act 1990, s 60(1): 'any ecclesiastical building which is for the time being used for ecclesiastical purposes'. A similar exemption is contained in the Planning Act (Northern Ireland) 2011, s 85(8).

[329] The heritage provisions in particular were amended by the Faculty Jurisdiction (Amendment) Rules 2019 with effect from 1st April 2020.

[330] Ecclesiastical Jurisdiction and Care of Churches Measure 2018 No 3, s. 56.

[331] Ecclesiastical Jurisdiction and Care of Churches Measure 2018 No 3, s. 58(1).(2).

[332] Ecclesiastical Jurisdiction and Care of Churches Measure 2018 No 3, s. 58(3),(4).

these do not include alterations which affect the special architectural or historic interest of the building in question or the sale or other disposal of an article of architectural, archaeological, artistic or historic interest.[333]

Otherwise a faculty is required and the Church courts may make orders, enforceable by contempt proceedings in the civil courts for the return of objects removed without authorization.[334]

Faculty decisions do have regard to the effect on the historic environment but also the Church of England's particular interests including the role of a church as a local centre of worship and mission.[335] A faculty may be granted subject to conditions.[336]

Faculty procedure

Where works are likely to affect the special architectural or historic interest of a church which is a listed building then pre-application consultation is required with Historic England, the local planning authority, the Church Buildings Council and such of the national amenity societies as appears to be likely to have an interest in the church or the works.[337] Consultation is also required with the Church Buildings Council if the works or proposals involve:[338]

> *"(a) the conservation, alteration or disposal of an article of special historic, architectural, archaeological or artistic interest;*

---

[333] Faculty Jurisdiction Rules 2015, rule 3.2, 3.3, Sched 1.

[334] A blistering warning to the art market was given by the Gloucester Consistory Court in *Emmanuel Church, Leckhampton*, 19 July 2014. The church had sought to sell a work by Franz Ittenbach (1813-1879), a German Nazarene painter; of a Madonna and Child without a faculty.

[335] Ecclesiastical Jurisdiction and Care of Churches Measure 2018 No 3, s. 35.

[336] Ecclesiastical Jurisdiction and Care of Churches Measure 2018 No 3, s. 68.

[337] Faculty Jurisdiction Rules 2015, rule 4.5, 4.6.

[338] Faculty Jurisdiction Rules 2015, rule 4.6(2).

(b) the introduction of an article of special historic, architectural, archaeological or artistic interest (including new work) in a grade I or II listed building;*

(c) the alteration, extension or re-ordering of a church in a way that is likely significantly to affect the setting of an article of special historic, architectural, archaeological or artistic interest; or

(d) the movement or removal of an article of special historic, architectural, archaeological or artistic interest such that the article might be adversely affected unless special precautions are taken."

The pre-application consultation period is 42 days.[339]

Proceedings are commenced by submitting a petition to the court at the diocesan registry.[340] Public notice of the petition must be displayed at the church or other building for 28 days.[341] Newspaper or website publication of the application may be required.[342] Historic England, the local planning authority and relevant national amenity societies will need to be consulted again, unless they had no objection or comment previously.[343] Unless they have previously been adequately consulted and given advice, the Church Buildings Council must be consulted on the petition.[344]

Objections may be made by interested persons being residents of the ecclesiastical parish, persons on the church electoral roll of the parish, the archdeacon, parochial church council, local planning authority, any national amenity society, any other person designated by the chancellor

[339] Faculty Jurisdiction Rules 2015, rule 4.8(4).

[340] Faculty Jurisdiction Rules 2015, rule 5.2.

[341] Faculty Jurisdiction Rules 2015, rule 6.3.

[342] Faculty Jurisdiction Rules 2015, rule 9.2. Website publication is required for certain works to listed buildings or demolition in conservation areas: Faculty Jurisdiction Rules 2015, rule 9.9.

[343] Faculty Jurisdiction Rules 2015, rule 9.3.

[344] Faculty Jurisdiction Rules 2015, rule 9.6.

and any person with a sufficient interest in the subject matter of the petition.[345]

Whilst a written representations procedure is available,[346] in *St Gregory's, Tredington*[347] the Arches Court considered that faculties for the sale of church treasures should seldom be granted without a hearing in open court.[348] Those heard as objectors are referred to as 'parties opponent'.

Orders

An interim faculty may be granted either in the course of a petition or upon an undertaking that a petition for a faculty will be submitted.[349] An injunction or restoration order may be sought by the archdeacon or any person with sufficient interest in the matter or made by the court[350] Interim injunctions may be granted.[351] The breach of an injunction or restoration order is a contempt of the consistory court. Matters that are a contempt of the consistory court may be sent by the presiding judge of the court to the High Court.[352] The High Court may then inquire into the allegation and hear evidence. It has the same powers as for dealing with contempt of the High Court,[353] including imposing a fine or imprisonment.

---

345 Faculty Jurisdiction Rules 2015, rule 10.1.

346 Faculty Jurisdiction Rules 2015, Part 14.

347 [1972] Fam. 236.

348 At 246. Endorsed in *St Lawrence, Oakley with Wotton St Lawrence* [2015] Fam. 27 at § 19. The Leeds Consistory Court said that written representations were appropriate when the items were not church treasures, there were no objections, expert consultees actively supported the petition and the parties consented to the procedure: *In re St James the Great, Flockton* [2016] P.T.S.R. 1290.

349 Faculty Jurisdiction Rules 2015, Part 15.

350 Faculty Jurisdiction Rules 2015, Part 16.

351 Faculty Jurisdiction Rules 2015, rule 16.6.

352 Ecclesiastical Jurisdiction and Care of Churches Measure 2018 No.3, s. 25(2),(3).

353 Ecclesiastical Jurisdiction and Care of Churches Measure 2018 No.3, s. 25(4).

The approach to faculties seeking approval for alterations and demolition

The Arches Court in *St Alkmund, Duffield*[354] suggested the following approach to proposed alterations to listed buildings:

> "*1. Would the proposals, if implemented, result in harm to the significance of the church as a building of special architectural or historic interest?*
>
> *2. If the answer to question (1) is "no", the ordinary presumption in faculty proceedings "in favour of things as they stand" is applicable, and can be rebutted more or less readily, depending on the particular nature of the proposals (see Peek v Trower (1881) 7 PD 21, 26-8, and the review of the case-law by Chancellor Bursell QC in In re St Mary's, White Waltham (No 2) [2010] PTSR 1689 at para 11). Questions 3, 4 and 5 do not arise.*
>
> *3. If the answer to question (1) is "yes", how serious would the harm be?*
>
> *4. How clear and convincing is the justification for carrying out the proposals?*
>
> *5. Bearing in mind that there is a strong presumption against proposals which will adversely affect the special character of a listed building (see St Luke, Maidstone*[355] *at p.8), will any resulting public benefit (including matters such as liturgical freedom, pastoral well-being, opportunities for mission, and putting the church to viable uses that are consistent with its role as a place of worship and mission) outweigh the harm? In answering question (5), the more serious the harm, the greater will be the level of benefit needed before the proposals should be permitted. This will particularly be the case if the harm is to a building which is listed Grade l or 2*, where serious harm should only exceptionally be allowed.*"

---

354 [2013] Fam 158, § 37. The approach in this case is referred to as the '*Duffield* guidelines'.

355 Author's note: [1995] Fam 1.

In *St John the Baptist, Penhurst*[356] the Court of Arches sought to clarify the guidelines:

> *"(a) Question 1 cannot be answered without prior consideration of what is the special architectural and/or historic interest of the listed church. That is why each of those matters was specifically addressed in Duffield , paras 57–58, the court having already found in para 52(i) that 'the chancellor fell into a material error in failing to identify what was the special character and historic interest of the church as a whole (including the appearance of the chancel) and then to consider whether there would be an overall adverse effect by reason of the proposed change'.*
>
> *(b) In answering questions 1 and 3, the particular grading of the listed church is highly relevant, whether or not serious harm will be occasioned. That is why in the Duffield case, para 56 the court's analysis of the effect on the character of the listed building referred to 'the starting point ... that this is a grade I listed building'.*
>
> *(c) In answering question 4, what matters are the elements which comprise the justification, including justification falling short of need or necessity: see the Duffield case, paras 85–86. That is why the document setting out the justification for the proposals is now described in rule 3.3(1)(b) of the 2013 Rules as a document commonly known as a 'statement of needs' (italics added), in recognition that it is not confined to needs strictly so-called.*
>
> *(d) Questions (1), (3) and (5) are directed at the effect of the works on the character of the listed building, rather than the effects of alteration, removal or disposal on a particular article."*

In *The Rustat Memorial, Jesus College, Cambridge*[357] the college authorities proposed to remove a memorial to a seventeenth century benefactor, Tobias Rustat, from the grade I listed chapel. Whilst contained in a secular college, the Chapel is included in the list of places

---

356 [2015] 3 WLUK 230, [2015] P.T.S.R. D40.

357 [2022] ECC Ely .

of worship[358] and so subject to the faculty jurisdiction and the ecclesiastical exemption. The judge, David Hodge QC, emphasised that the secular heritage principles are not applied in precisely the same way as "*a church (or a college chapel) is a house of God and a place for worship: it does not belong to conservationists, to the state, or to the congregation, but rather to God.*"[359]

Tobias Rustat (baptised 1608, died 1694) was a principal benefactor of the college. He had commissioned the memorial, almost certainly from the studio of Grinling Gibbons, to be installed in the Chapel following his death.[360] The memorial comprised hand-carved marble, 2.6 metres high and 1.6 metres wide, weighing about 3.5 tonnes and containing a portrait and inscription.

The college contended that any harm caused to the significance of the Chapel as a building of special architectural and historic interest by the removal of the Rustat memorial was substantially outweighed by the resulting public benefits, in terms of pastoral well-being and opportunities for mission. The college's petition was dismissed. The removal would cause considerable harm to the listed building[361] and the removal of the memorial was not necessary to enable the Chapel to play its proper role in providing a credible Christian ministry and witness to the college community, or for it to act as a focus for secular activities and events in the wider life of the college.[362] The judge found that the opposition to the memorial was based on a "*false narrative*" that Rustat had amassed much of his wealth from the slave trade, and that it was

---

358 The list being maintained by the Church Buildings Council under *Ecclesiastical Jurisdiction and Care of Churches Measure,* s. 38.

359 [2022] ECC Ely 2 at para 5. The importance of the beauty and history of churches was emphasised in *Re All Saints, Hooton Pagnell* [2017] ECC She 1 at § 20 per Chancellor Singleton QC.

360 The memorial remained the property of Rustat's heirs-at-law: see § 40 per David Hodge QC.

361 At § 123.

362 *Rustat Memorial* at § 6, 125, 126. It was noted that the community involved in a college chapel would be wider than that for a parish: see § 121.

moneys from this source that he used to benefit the college.[363] In practice he had little return from his investment in two slave trading companies, and that was long after his contributions to the college. Rustat is buried in the Chapel. The judge suggested that appropriate interpretation and explanation would enable "*the Rustat memorial [to be] employed as an appropriate vehicle to consider the imperfection of human beings and to recognise that none of us is free from all sin; and to question our own lives, as well as Rustat's, asking whether, by (for example) buying certain clothes or other consumer goods, or eating certain foods, or investing in the companies that produce them, we are ourselves contributing to, or supporting, conditions akin to modern slavery*".[364]

The approach to faculties seeking approval for the removal of objects

The faculty jurisdiction extends to objects within a church even if they are not attached to the building. To that degree it goes beyond listed building control. Church treasures are 'articles of architectural, archaeological, artistic or historic interest'[365] and may include secular objects deposited in churches for devotional or other reasons.[366] In *St Lawrence, Oakley with Wootton St Lawrence* the Arches Court of Canterbury considered the attempted sale of an armet, a type of helmet dating from around 1500. This had been part of the funerary monument to Sir Thomas Hooke, who died in 1677. The chancellor had held that it remained the property of the heirs of Sir Thomas, not the church.[367] Objects within a church are subject to the faculty jurisdiction even if they are owned by another person.[368]

[363] See § 129

[364] At § 8, and see § 133.

[365] *In re St Peter, Shipton Bellinger* [2016] Fam. 163 at § 3.

[366] *St Lawrence, Oakley with Wootton St Lawrence* [2015] Fam. 27.

[367] *St Lawrence* § 20.

[368] *In re Escot Church* [1979] Fam 125, at p. 127.

In *St Lawrence* the armet had been removed to a bank vault in 1969 for safekeeping.[369] It was then loaned to the Armouries of the Tower of London (with a faculty). In 2010 an unopposed faculty was granted for the sale of the armet with a condition "*Subject to the possibility of a prior satisfactory and acceptable offer being made by the Royal Armouries or some other British museum or institution, the helmet shall be sold on the open market for the best possible price*". Following its sale at auction matters unravelled. The 2010 faculty had been granted in breach of the requirement to consult the Church Buildings Council. The CBC successfully applied to set aside the faculty.[370] They also said that the consent of the heirs was required. Two heirs were traced, one of whom gifted his ownership to the churchwardens whilst the other insisted upon receiving his half of the proceeds.[371]

A new faculty was refused by the Arches Court.

The Arches Court considered that there was a strong presumption against the sale of church treasures and the question is whether the grounds for sale are sufficiently compelling to outweigh this strong presumption.[372] If disposal is contemplated then a sequential approach should be taken. The first is to consider disposal by loan to a museum, art gallery or diocesan treasury. Such a loan is preferable to long-term deposit in a bank vault. A loan will need a faculty and is likely to be sanctioned[373] (although this latter comment must be qualified if the removal will affect any special historic or architectural interest of the church). Ranking second in the sequence would be a "*disposal by limited sale*" to a museum, art gallery or (more rarely) diocesan treasury, but still subject to the strong

---

369 Without the necessary faculty, *St Lawrence* at §28.

370 *St Lawrence* §15.

371 A 'monument' which includes a tomb, gravestone or other memorial, is owned by the person who erected it or after that person's death, the heir or heirs at law of the person or persons in whose memory the monument was erected: Ecclesiastical Jurisdiction and Care of Churches Measure 2018 No.3, s.66(5).

372 At §§ 51 and 91.

373 At §34(a).

presumption against. The final route would be disposal by outright sale, a sale on the open market.[374]

In *St James the Great, Flockton*[375] it was said by the consistory court that the strict *St Lawrence* approach should apply only to church treasures.

In May 2021 the Church Buildings Council and the Cathedrals Fabric Commission for England published statutory guidance entitled *'Contested Heritage in Churches and Cathedrals'*.[376] It advises that:[377]

> *"In terms of attempting to justify a physical intervention such as altering or removing a memorial what needs to be proven is not principally that a memorial is to somebody (or perhaps donated by somebody) whose views or actions we would now condemn, but rather that the presence of the memorial has a demonstrable negative impact on the mission and ministry of the church or cathedral; and, in the case of a proposed course of action that may be considered harmful to the heritage of a building, that substantially the same benefits could not be achieved by a less harmful option."*

Cathedrals

Cathedrals and their precincts are governed by a separate regime the Care of Cathedrals Measure 2011 No.1. Approval is required for works affecting the architectural, archaeological, artistic or historic character of the cathedral church or any ecclesiastical building within its precinct:[378]

> *"(b) for the sale, loan or other disposal of any object of architectural, archaeological, artistic or historic interest vested in or in the possession*

[374] See §§34 and 36.

[375] [2016] P.T.S.R. 1290.

[376] Under Care of Cathedrals Measure 2011, s. 3(3)(a) and Dioceses, Mission and Pastoral Measure 2007, s. 55(1)(d). The guidance was described as 'helpful and considered' in *Rustat Mermorial* at § 127 per David Hodge QC.

[377] Agreed in *Rustat Memorial* at § 128.

[378] Care of Cathedrals Measure 2011 No.1, s. 2.

or custody of the cathedral or which it is entitled to have possession of, or

(d) for the permanent addition to the cathedral church of any object which would materially affect the architectural, archaeological, artistic or historic character of the cathedral church."

Applications are determined either by the Cathedrals Fabric Commission for England or the fabric advisory committee for the cathedral.[379] All applications made to the Commission are publicized by notice, including notice to the fabric advisory committee, Historic England and the national amenity societies. Additionally applications for works within s. 2(1)(a) are notified to the local planning authority.[380] The Church Commissioners and the Council of the cathedral may also be consulted on proposals for the sale, loan or disposal of objects (other than human remains).[381] The Commission's jurisdiction includes the sale, loan or other disposal of or the carrying out of any work to any object for the time being designated in relation to the cathedral church as being of outstanding architectural, archaeological, artistic or historic interest.

---

[379] Care of Cathedrals Measure 2011 No.1, s. 6.

[380] Care of Cathedrals Measure 2011 No.1, s. 9(1).

[381] Care of Cathedrals Measure 2011 No.1, s. 9(4), (5).

PART TWO

OWNERSHIP

OVERVIEW

In this Part, Chapter 7 will look at the question of how personal property becomes incorporated as part of the land. The distinction between personal property and real property affects not only which rule set should be applied, but also who owns the heritage asset in question.

Chapter 8 then considers the tort of conversion. English law gives protection to legal title in personal property through tort law: one of the most important of those torts in this field is the tort of conversion.

Chapter 9 then looks at how heritage assets are conveyed from one person to another, especially by sale.

'Ownership' is a troubled concept in English law, which has preferred to deal with the question of possession. On one conception of ownership, it is a description of a collection of rights held by persons over physical and other things.[382] As part of that collection, or bundle, of rights, the right of enjoyment and the right of disposal are central features.[383]

The private law ownership of an object, therefore, carries with it (alongside other rights) the right to enjoy that object and the right to dispose of it. What ownership gives a party, therefore, is control in respect of the object.

Ownership may not, however, be single in an object, especially when it comes to real property in English law. While it may be possible to conceive of absolute ownership in a chattel, with only one party capable of being able of possessing or selling it, this is not the case in real property. The closest one may get to this is a fee simple absolute in possession, or the freehold estate. This may, however, be subject to a trust of land, when it comes to co-ownership; or to a leasehold estate that is carved out of the

---

382 *Yearworth v North Bristol NHS Trust* [2010] Q.B. 1 at §28, *per* Lord Judge CJ.

383 See also Tony Honoré's influential discussion, identifying eleven facets of ownership, in "Ownership" in Guest, A.G., (ed), *Oxford Essays in Jurisprudence [First Series]* (1961).

freehold estate; or other proprietary interests in the estate, such as a mortgage, an easement or a restrictive covenant. This complicates the way in which we conceive of how art and cultural property may be removed. Some examples, based on the cases that will be considered in this Part, illustrate these complications.

> Example 1: The landlord, A, leases a flat to B. B installs wood paneling, fireplaces and chimney pieces. B now wishes to remove these objects, but A objects, arguing that they have become part of the freehold (*Spyer v Phillipson* [1931] 2 Ch 183).

> Example 2: A is the owner of a large country house, Greenacre Hall. A wants to sell the house itself separately from the paintings and the sculptures in the house and gardens. At auction, B buys the land at Greenacre Hall from A. Unknown to B, A then sells paintings which have been installed in wood panelling and a substantial statute in the grounds. B claims the value of these items, arguing that they have been conveyed to him together with Greenacre Hall (*Berkley v Poulett* [1977] 1 EGLR 86).

> Example 3: As part of a building scheme, A intends to install a work of art. Following the design of the building scheme, A acquires a sculpture from a well-known artist. The land on which the building scheme and the sculpture stands is, in due course, vested in B, but C acquires A's interest in all of its other assets. B now seeks to sell the sculpture. (*Tower Hamlets LBC v Bromley LBC* [2015] EWHC 1954 (Ch)).

In each of these examples, we have a dispute between two parties who can legitimately claim to have 'ownership' rights. In the case of Example 1, both A and B can claim to have an interest in the disputed objects. In Example 2, the dispute will turn on what was sold to B. In Example 3, the dispute might well turn on whether that sculpture became part of the land or whether it remained a free-standing object or chattel.

The question of 'ownership' is not an arid academic debate: it is a serious issue for the management and curatorship of collections. Material may have been acquired illegally or immorally. Some items are expensive to preserve. It can be difficult to house a growing collection. The sale of some of those items may be difficult without confidence that the collector or museum actually has the title to sell them. It might well be the case that the property itself was provided on trust for the museum, imposing restrictions on the museum's ability to deal with the property.[384] Property, therefore, gives its owner control, but might equally impose liability on that owner.

[384] Janet Ulph, 'The Sale of Items in Museum Collections' in *Modern Studies in Property Law* (vol. 7) ed. Nicholas Hopkins (Hart, 2013), 217.

CHAPTER SEVEN

ANNEXATION TO THE LAND

The most contentious private law issue when removing art or other property from a building is whether the object is personal property, or whether it has instead become part of the building itself. This can radically affect the ownership of the object itself. An object on loan to a stately home, for example, will remain the property of the lender, unless it becomes annexed to the land itself; at this point, the owner of the land will acquire it (potentially becoming liable in the tort of conversion, which is discussed in the following chapter).

The rules as to when an object becomes part of the land are some of the most heavily criticised in English land law, which has been described as "*erratic and unpredictable*".[385] This is particularly the case when it comes to art and cultural property. While it is relatively straightforward to identify the high-level principles, in borderline cases it is extremely difficult to identify which legal analyses or presumptions will be applied to decide a particular case.

This chapter will consider the following.

(1) Firstly, it will consider the distinction between an object that is taken on to land, but which remains personal property, and an object that does become part of the land.

(2) It will then consider the general legal test as to how an object becomes part of the land.

---

385 Chris Bevan, 'The law of fixtures and chattels: recalibration, rationalisation and reform' (2021) Legal Studies 1, 5.

(3) The chapter will then consider the status of fixtures which become part of the land, but which are subject to a right of removability.

(4) It will then consider how these general tests have been applied in cases involving heritage assets, and in particular, the question of architectural design. The way in which these cases were discussed in *Dill* will also be referred to.

The distinction between an object that remains personal property and an object that becomes part of the land

The term 'land' does not simply refer to the ground that buildings or objects may stand on. By s. 205(1)(ix) of the Law of Property Act 1925, the term 'land' includes "*buildings or parts of buildings (whether the division is horizontal, vertical or made in any other way) and other corporeal hereditaments*". If an object 'becomes part' of the land (such as when bricks and mortar are used to build a brick wall), then it is treated as being land.

English law, like many other jurisdictions, adopts a different set of rules when it comes to how land ownership is dealt with when compared to personal property.

Furthermore, when land is bought, sold, leased or otherwise disposed of or dealt with, the general rule is that objects which are part of the land are disposed of at the same time. Section 62(1) of the Law of Property Act 1925 confirms that "*A conveyance of land shall be deemed to include and shall by virtue of this Act operate to convey, with the land, all buildings, erections, fixtures...*".

The circumstances in which an object remains personal property, or when it becomes part of the land, are therefore highly significant. The general rule can be stated that, '*quicquid plantatur, solo cedit*' ('whatever is attached to the soil becomes part of it').[386]

If an object, such as a statue or other piece of art, is brought on to land, it falls into one of three broad heads.[387]

(1) It might remain a chattel, or personal property. The ownership of the object is subject to the rules pertaining to personal property, which are dealt with in the next two chapters. If the object remains a chattel, then the mere fact that it is brought on to the land does not change its ownership.

(2) The object might become a fixture, that is part of the land.

(3) The object is treated as part and parcel of the land.

Objects that fall into heads (2) and (3), therefore, become part of the land. Questions of ownership are dealt with pursuant to the rules pertaining to real property. It is those rules that are considered in the first part of this chapter.

There is, therefore, a further distinction in respect of objects which become part of the land. In respect of some objects, certain parties retain a right to remove the object, even though it has become part of the land. The rules that govern the distinction between objects which are always part of the land, and objects subject to a right of removal, is sometimes known as the law of fixtures. These rules are often technical and have been subject to sustained academic criticism. This rule set will be considered in the last part of this chapter.

If an object becomes part of the land, then the person who owns the land also 'owns' the object (subject to rights to remove the object by the person who owned the personal property in it). If, for example, I erect an art installation that is permanently installed on another person's land so that

---

[386] *Minshall v Lloyd* (1837) 2 M & W 450 at 459; *Elliott v Bishop* (1854) 10 Ex 496 at p. 507.

[387] Lord Browne-Wilkinson in *Elitestone Ltd v Morris* [1997] 1 WLR 687 at p. 691H, citing *Woodfall's Landlord and Tenant*, vol. 1, § 13.131.

it becomes part of their land, I lose any rights of ownership that I may have in it, and in turn, they now own it as part of their land.[388] The question of whether an object has become part of the land, therefore, will often determine the question of ownership between competing claimants.[389]

How does an object become part of land?

The distinction between what is personal property, and when personal property becomes part of the land, has considerable significance in a number of respects, both in respect of art and contested heritage, but in other spheres such as housing, lending, and construction. The general rules that have developed have arisen from a series of cases with often very different factual situations, which apart from the general question of the threshold between personal property and real property, appear to have little to do with each other. Consequently, while the general test is initially fairly easy to state, the different factors that point in different directions are less easy to apply in practice. The following sub-section will consider the general test, before cases which are related to art and heritage are discussed. Finally, the important and interesting decision of Norris J in the *Tower Hamlets LBC v Bromley LBC* ("*Tower Hamlets*") will be discussed.

The general test

The leading case that re-stated the general rule is the House of Lords decision in *Elitestone Ltd v Morris* ("*Elitestone*").[390] The plaintiffs owned the freehold of the land. A number of wooden bungalows had been erected on that land. One of them was occupied by the defendants, Mr and Mrs Morris, who occupied it in return for an annual payment. Those bungalows rested on concrete pillars without being attached to them. The bungalows could only be removed by demolishing them. The question

[388] *Melluish v BMI (No 3)* [1996] AC 454 at p. 473.

[389] Stuart Bridge, Elizabeth Cooke and Martin Dixon, *Megarry & Wade The Law of Real Property* (9th edition, Sweet & Maxwell), § 22-005.

[390] [1997] 1 WLR 687.

was therefore whether they were personal property, which did not attract any protection under housing legislation, or were buildings (and hence real property).

When the plaintiffs sought to obtain possession, the court at first instance held that they were dwellings that were protected by the Rent Act 1977 ("the Rent Act"), and refused to order possession. The Court of Appeal reversed the decision. It was held that the bungalows were personal property. The occupier fell outside the protection of the Rent Act. As a result, the plaintiffs were entitled to possession. The House of Lords allowed the appeal and held that the first instance decision was correct: the bungalow was a part of the land, Mr and Mrs Morris were protected by the Rent Act, and they could not be evicted.

Lord Lloyd gave one of the main speeches in the House of Lords. As with the other members of the House of Lords, he referred back to *Holland v Hodgson* (which was itself a mortgage lending case),[391] and the two factors that Blackburn J had identified, namely (1) the degree of annexation to the land, and (2) the object of annexation. When considering whether an object has become part of the land, it is necessary in all cases to refer back to these two factors.

(1) Degree of annexation to the land

This is a reference to how firmly an object is attached to the land. In the case of a substantial building, such as a house or warehouse, there may be little dispute about the degree to which it is annexed to the land: if there is any dispute over an object such as this, it tends to turn on the object of annexation.

Not all houses or other 'buildings' are fixed to the land. Lord Lloyd in *Elitestone* referred to the decision of the High Court of Australia in *Reid v Smith*,[392] where a house resting on its own weight (i.e. not attached) to brick piers to prevent an invasion of white ants was considered to become part of the land. On the other hand, as discussed in the leading case of

391 (1872) LR 7 CP 328.

392 (1903) 3 CLR 656.

Mitchell v Cowie from the Court of Appeal in Trinidad and Tobago, a kind of house known as a chattel house was considered to fall into two categories: the first where the structure rested on its own weight on a stone or brick base, which remained a chattel and therefore could be removed by the tenant, and a house which was affixed in some way, which became part of the land.[393] Notwithstanding this, in the Bahamian case of *O'Brien Loans Ltd v Missick*, even though a house resting on wooden beams showed a considerable degree of annexation, the Court of Appeal of the Bahamas held that the purpose of annexation indicated that the yearly tenant of the plot of land on which it stood had no intention of adding value to the land, and hence it remained a chattel.[394]

The analogy referred to by Lord Lloyd in *Elitestone* was the example given by Blackburn J in *Holland v Hodgson* of a dry stone wall. Even though the blocks of stone do not have mortar or cement connecting them to the ground, on account of the purpose or object of annexation, they become part of the land; the same stones deposited in a builder's yard and stored in the form of a wall, however, remain chattels.[395]

Even if an object has been lightly attached to the land, it is appropriate to consider whether the object cab be removed as a whole or not; whether it can be removed easily; and whether it can be removed without causing damage to the object itself or the fabric of the building it is attached to.[396] If, therefore, a building is easily demountable, this points to it remaining a chattel.[397]

The degree of annexation, therefore, is an important factor, but not decisive. It might well be better to regard it as establishing a presumption that an object that is annexed to the land has become part of it, but subject to the object of that annexation: "*Perhaps the true rule is that*

---

393 (1964) 7 WIR 118

394 (1977) 1 BLR 49.

395 *Elitestone* , p. 693; *Holland v Hodgson,* p. 335.

396 *Hellawell v Eastwood* (1851) 6 Exch. 295, p. 312, Parke B., approved by Lord Clyde in *Elitestone*, p. 696. Note that the result, but not Parke B.'s reasoning, was overturned in *Holland v Hodgson* (1872) LR 7 CP 328.

397 *Deen v Andrews* [1986] 262, as discussed by Lord Clyde in *Elitestone v Morris*, 699.

articles not otherwise attached to the land than by their own weight are not to be considered as part of the land unless the circumstances are such as to show that they were intended to be part of the laud, the onus of showing that they are so intended lying on those who assert that they have ceased to be chattels; and that, on the contrary, an article which is affixed to the land, even slightly, is to be, considered as part of the land, unless the circumstances are such as to show that it was intended all along to continue a chattel, the onus lying on those who contend that it is a chattel."[398] It has been said that the test of degree of annexation has become subordinate to the test of purpose.[399]

(2) The object of annexation

The subjective intention of the parties is irrelevant. The intention of the parties can only be derived from the degree and object of the annexation.[400] This was confirmed in the House of Lords decision in *Melluish v BMI (No 3) Ltd.*[401] As a result, even if the parties declare in an agreement such as a conveyance that an object is not to become part of the land, this will have no effect on whether or not it has, in fact, become part of the land. This was shown most graphically in the decision in *Hobson v Gorringe*,[402] where a gas engine was let out on hire purchase. The agreement said that the engine would not become the property of the hirer until all instalments had been paid; the engine itself had a hire plate on it. The argument that the engine always remained a chattel was rejected: it was held that it had become a fixture when it was annexed to the land. The only relevant intention was that which can be objectively ascertained from circumstances patent for all to see, which showed the degree of annexation and the object of such annexation, and not to the

[398] *Holland v Hodgson,* 335 *per* Blackburn J.

[399] *Hamp v Bygrave* [1983] 1 EGLR 174 at p. 177, *per* Boreham J.

[400] *Elitestone*, p. 693 *per* Lord Lloyd.

[401] [1996] AC 154.

[402] [1897] 1 Ch 182.

circumstances of the agreement between an owner of a chattel and its hirer.[403]

Lord Lloyd also noted "*Many different tests have been suggested, such as whether the object which has been fixed to the property has been so fixed for the better enjoyment of the object as a chattel, or whether it has been fixed with a view to effecting a permanent improvement of the freehold*". This was less applicable to a house, but it comes into its own when considering works of art, which we shall return to.

Lord Clyde, like Blackburn J, referred back to the decision in *Hellawell v Eastwood* with approval.[404] Baron Parke in that case had asked whether an object could be removed integré, salve et commode, and if not, without injury to itself or the fabric of the building. The fact that the bungalow was not removable in one piece, and that it was not demountable for erection elsewhere, was a powerful indication it was not of the nature of a chattel.

Lord Clyde also emphasised that, when considering the purpose of annexation, 'intention' is to be considered objectively: it is the purpose which the object is serving which has to be regarded, not the purpose of the person who put it there.

The difference between 'part and parcel of the land' and objects which can be removed

The term 'fixture' is used in different situations and is apt to cause misunderstand and confusion, as Lord Lloyd noted in *Elitestone*.[405] As Lord Clyde noted in that case, a clear distinction has to be drawn between the principle of accession (by which objects become part of the land) and the rules of removability.[406] When reading some of the cases, it is necessary to take care to ensure whether the dispute concerns

403 *Hobson v Gorringe* [1897] 1 Ch 182 at p. 193 *per* Lord Blackburn.

404 (1851) 6 Exch. 295.

405 *Elitestone*, p. 691.

406 Ibid, p. 695.

'removability' on account of the object remaining a chattel, or because the person who affixed an object which has become part of the land nevertheless retained a right to remove it.[407]

The most commonly encountered exception is in respect of tenant's fixtures installed for the purpose of trade. Legal title to the fixture remains in the landlord; however, the tenant has a power to remove items which are properly fixtures (as opposed to being part and parcel of the land) during the tenancy or, in cases of forfeiture or surrender, within a reasonable period of time after the end of the tenancy.[408]

By the end of the nineteenth century, however, a further exception was recognized in respect of objects affixed to the freehold by way of ornament.[409] In the early case of *Martin v Roe*, it was considered that an erection that was purely a matter of ornament, so that it was a chattel attached for the purpose of completing an ornamental creation, could be removed so long as it could be detached without injury to the freehold.[410] This case, as with the case of *Leigh v Taylor* (discussed below), make reference to the object never ceasing to be a chattel. The authors of *Megarry & Wade,* however, state that such an object is better explained as a fixture (and not an 'annexed chattel) which a tenant can remove.[411] This is also consistent with the three-fold classification endorsed in *Elitestone.*

One clear illustration of the importance of the 'ornamental and domestic fixtures' exception was *Spyer v Phillipson.*[412] The lessee of a flat had installed valuable antique oak and pine panelling, chimney pieces and fireplaces. The landlord argued that they were landlord's fixtures, and

---

[407] So, for example, in *Webb v Frank* [1940] 1 All ER 24, the object in question was a large shed was a fixture (i.e. it became part of the land) that was removable by the tenant.

[408] *Ex p. Brook* (1878) 10 Ch D 100.

[409] *Elitestone*, pp. 695-6; Re De Falbe [1901] 1 Ch 523; *Leigh v Taylor* [1902] AC 157.

[410] (1857) 7 E & B 237; 119 ER 1235.

[411] *Megarry & Wade*, § 22-015.

[412] [1931] 2 Ch 183.

hence could not be removed by the tenant. Luxmoore J, at first instance, noted the general rule that whatever is affixed during the currency of the lease to the freehold forms part of that freehold and cannot be removed unless it falls within certain well known exceptions. He held that the tenant did not have the object of making a gift of the items to the landlord, and that the method of attachment was slight. The Court of Appeal agreed with Luxmoore J's judgment that the tenant could remove the items.

The art cases

D'Eyncourt v Gregory (1866) LR 3 Eq 382

One of the earliest cases of continuing significance is the decision of Lord Romilly, MR in *D'Eyncourt v Gregory*.[413] The testator, Mr Gregory Gregory, was the tenant for life of a number of estates under the will of George De Ligne Gregory; he was also the tenant in fee simple of other states. He built in what was described as "*on a large and magnificent scale*" the manor house of Harlaxton, in Lincolnshire, in substitution for the old one which had fallen into decay, and partially furnished it. The manor remains a notable piece of architecture, being a grade I listed building, and the British campus of the University of Evansville. Gregory Gregory bequeathed all the tapestry, marbles, statues, pictures with their frames and glasses, which should be in or about the house at the time of his death, and of which he had power to dispose, to be enjoyed as heir-looms by the persons who, under the limitations in his will, would be entitled to his own estates, subject to a condition. This condition was not, however, fulfilled, so that the settled estate devolved to one person, but another became entitled to the devised estates and the heir-looms. When Gregory Gregory died, the issue was, who received what? This turned on which of the articles more or less closely attached to the house were removable, and which were not removable.

In what Lord Romilly, MR accepted was a difficult decision, he held that the tapestry put up by Gregory Gregory took the place of panelling or a

---

[413] (1866) LR 3 Eq 382.

fresco painting, and therefore could not be considered to be removable fixtures. Likewise, a painting was considered to be a wall covering. As set out below, these parts of the decision have not been followed.

The most enduring part of the decision concerned carved kneeling figures in the staircase of the great hall and the sculptured marble vases in the hall. Lord Romilly, MR, again, held they could not be removed. This did "*not depend on whether any cement is used for fixing these articles, or whether they rest by their own weight*". Instead, the test was whether "*they are strictly and properly part of the architectural design for the hall and staircase itself, and put in there as such, as distinguished from mere ornaments to be afterwards added.*"[414] This was comparable to the stone of a mill, which is part of the mill itself. He himself accepted that the test was difficult to apply:

> "*I admit that the distinction between such statues as are added by way of ornament, and such as belong to an architectural design, and form part of the design itself, is extremely thin, and that in many cases it would be difficult to distinguish them, unless it were done in an arbitrary manner, so closely might one run into the other. But I am unable to suggest any other mode by which the true construction can be defined more accurately than that which I have already stated.*"[415]

Aspects of the case have been doubted in subsequent decisions. The Court of Appeal in *Re De Falbe,* for example, disapproved of the decision.[416] The test as to architectural design has, however, found continuing support.[417]

---

[414] Ibid, p. 396.

[415] Ibid, pp.396-7.

[416] [1901] 1 Ch 523, at 531-2; on appeal, this was *Leigh v Taylor* [1902] AC 157. In *Dill,* Lord Carnwath noted the doubtful nature of the authority at §40 and the criticisms that had been made in *In re De Falbe.*

[417] See, for example, the reference by Lord Clyde to the sculptures in this case that "*simply rested by their own weight were held to form part of the architectural design for the hall in which they were placed and so fell to be treated as part of the freehold*" in *Elitestone* at p. 697.

Leigh v Taylor [1902] AC 157

In *Leigh v Taylor*, tapestries were hung in the drawing-room of the mansion house of the Luton Hoo Estates by Madame de Falbe. She was a tenant for life; she therefore did not own the freehold, but only had a life interest in the property. The tapestries were hung by stretching them over canvas, and affixing them with tacks; mouldings fastened to the wall were placed round each piece of tapestry. When Madame de Falbe died, the question was whether the tapestries had become part of the land, therefore passing to the remainderman, or whether they remained chattels, and hence belonging to the estate of Madame de Falbe. At first blush, all of the fixtures would have to be left to the remainderman,[418] subject to the question of the common law exception for ornamental and domestic fixtures.

The Court of Appeal (in *In Re de Falbe*) held that the tapestries had been affixed for the purpose of ornamentation and the better enjoyment of them as chattels.[419] Consequently, on the death of the tenant for life, they did not pass with the freehold to the remainderman, but formed part of the personal estate of Madame de Falbe and could be removed by her executor. Rigby LJ noted that the 'trade fixture' exception had been extended to the case of the tenant for life. He also observed that objects fixed to the freehold, not with the object of enhancing its value, but for purposes of ornamentation, were also removable. He had considerable doubt about the conclusion of Lord Romilly MR as to the status of the tapestries.[420] Vaughan Williams LJ, as well, confirmed that an exception applied in respect of ornamental fixtures as between the executor and the heir.[421] He also noted that, in order to enjoy some heavy chattels (such as an ormolu clock) it was necessary to employ substantial fixings. In many cases, this kind of fixing would be conclusive of an incorporation of the chattel with the freehold: "*But, the moment you come to the conclusion that the mode of fixing which was employed was absolutely*

---

[418] *Lawton v Lawton* (1743) 3 Atk. 13.

[419] [1901] 1 Ch 523.

[420] Ibid, pp. 531-2.

[421] Ibid, 535-6.

necessary for the enjoyment of the chattel, that inference does not arise."[422] He agreed that the tapestries had been hung for their own enjoyment, and that this accounted for the manner in which they had been attached to the walls. Stirling LJ also agreed that there was an exception in respect of ornamental objects, and that this was included as between the tenant for life and remaindermen.[423]

The House of Lords in *Leigh v Taylor* upheld the decision of the Court of Appeal. Lord Halsbury considered whether when the tapestries had been attached to the walls they had been intended to become part of the realty, or whether this was only a "*mode of enjoyment of the thing while the person is temporarily there*".[424] The nature of Madame de Falbe's interest in the land was regarded as a highly material factor: as he asked, "*is it conceivable that a person would for the purpose of a tenancy from year to year put up these things exactly in this way if thereby they made a present of 7000l to the landlord?*".[425] He considered that the only purpose of the tapestries was ornamentation or decoration. The wall had not been affected in any significant way by their affixation: they were only slightly attached. It was held that they were never intended to become a part of the house. As Lord Macnaghten also observed, the mode of annexation was only one of the circumstances of the case.

The House of Lords, therefore, upheld the decision of the Court of Appeal that objects set up for the purpose of decoration or ornamentation are excepted from the rule that things fixed to the freehold belong to the owner of the freehold.[426] Instead, as an "*ornamental fixture*", it could be removed by whoever had the right to put up the chattel.

Berkley v Poulett [1977] 1 EGLR 86

This case illustrates one of the scenarios when the difference between real property and personal property or chattels is of critical importance. The

---

422 Ibid, 536.

423 Ibid, pp. 539-540.

424 *Leigh v Taylor* [1902] AC 157, p. 158.

425 Ibid, p. 159.

426 *Re De Falbe* [1901] 1 Ch 523, p. 534 *per* Rigby LJ.

case concerned objects in Hinton House, near Hinton St George in Somerset. It was owned by successive Lords Poulett, whose family lived in the house for some 500 years. The south wing was said to have been designed by Inigo Jones. It was built for the reception of Queen Anne who, in fact, never arrived. It contained two rooms of importance to the case: the Queen's Dining Room, and the Queen's Ante-Room.

In the Queen's Dining Room there were six pictures, firmly fixed into recesses in the panelling of the room. In the Queen's Ante-Room, there were a number of pictures, two of which were affixed to a wall. Finally, in the grounds, there were two objects that were also subject to the ensuing dispute: a white marble statue of a Greek athlete, weighing approximately half a ton and standing on a plinth which was fixed into position on the West Lawn; and a sundial which rested on a stone baluster (or pedestal) outside the South Wing.

Lord Poulet, the eighth Earl, decided to put up for sale by public auction the ancestral estate, including Hinton House as part of the sale. Hinton House with its gardens, grounds and entrance lodge was lot 1. In the event, the plaintiff, Mr Berkley, acquired the house by way of a subsale at the auction. The Earl had in mind, however, selling the contents of the house separately. After the auction, five of the six paintings were taken from the Queen's Dining Room and sold. The sundial was also removed, while the statue was listed for sale. Ultimately, all of the disputed items were removed before Mr Berkley completed on the purchase of the House. The question for the Court of Appeal, therefore, was if the pictures, statue or sundial were fixtures (i.e. part of the land).

Scarman LJ, with whom Stamp LJ agreed, held that the items were fixtures; Goff LJ dissented. Scarman LJ referred back to *Leigh v Taylor*, noting that the question whether objects which were chattels have become part of the freehold, depends upon the application of two tests: (1) the method and degree of annexation; (2) the object and purpose of the annexation.[427] As he noted, the degree of annexation had fallen in terms of importance as a factor: depending on the facts, it may prove nothing. He observed that, "*If the purpose of the annexation be for the better*

[427] *Berkley v Poulett* [1977] 1 EGLR 86, p. 88.

enjoyment of the object itself, it may remain a chattel, notwithstanding a high degree of physical annexation."[428] If, however, an object cannot be removed without serious damage to, or destruction of, some part of the realty, then there is a strong case for it having become a fixture. On the other hand, an object, resting on the ground by its own weight alone, can be a fixture, if it be so heavy that there is no need to tie it into a foundation, and if it were put in place to improve the realty. He cited Neville J in *In Re Whaley* in support of the proposition that an object affixed to realty but capable of being removed without much difficulty may be a fixture, if, for example, the purpose of its affixing be that "*of creating a beautiful room as a whole*".[429]

In respect of the pictures, Scarman LJ regarded the decisive question to be the object and purpose of their affixing. He regarded it to be more plausible that when the panelling was installed in the two rooms, the design was for panelled walls with recesses for pictures to be enjoyed as pictures, and not as rooms having walls which were a composite of panelling and pictures. There was no unity of design (unlike, for example, the Elizabeth Room in *In Re Whaley*).

As for the statue, it was cemented in, but it was easily removable. Scarman LJ considered that it was the position of the plinth on which the statute rested, not the object on the plinth, that was of central importance. Previously, a sundial had stood on the plinth. The plinth's position was important, "*But the object it carried could be whatever appealed to the occupier for the time being.*" The sundial, as well, had been detached many years before; once it had been detached, it ceased to be part of the realty.

Goff LJ dissented. He would regard the statue and the sundial has having not been placed there for their better enjoyment as chattels, but for the permanent enhancement of the beauty of the grounds. Whether or not the statue was cemented in, he regarded the fact that it rested upon its own bulk as sufficient annexation. The critical point for Goff LJ was that *De Falbe* and *Leigh v Taylor* were concerned with removable fixtures. He

---

[428] Ibid.

[429] [1908] 1 Ch 615 at p. 619. See also *Lord Chesterfield's Settled Estates* [1911] 1 Ch 237.

considered, in particular, the Queen's Ante Room pictures were removable fixtures but that the Queen's Dining Room were not. His dissenting judgment illustrates the difficulty caused by the distinction between chattels, fixtures and objects which become part and parcel of the land.

This remains the leading case when it comes to the question of whether an object such as a painting has become a fixture. It is, however, hard to discern a clear rationale from the case. Undoubtedly, a picture is hung both to allow it to be enjoyed, *and* to better enhance the room it is displayed in. Stamp LJ preferred to decide the case on the basis that oil pictures tend to remain chattels in character.

When, therefore, Newey J considered the question of the status of oil paintings housed in Savernake Lodge in *Earl of Cadogan v Moore*,[430] he referred back to the two-fold test set out in *Holland v Hodgson* and *Berkley v Poulett*, and cited Stamp LJ's observations that "*Framed pictures are hung on or fixed to the walls for their better enjoyment as pictures, however much they may beautify the rooms in which they are found*", and "*Framed oil paintings in my judgment are, and remain, chattels whether they be hung upon, or over, or screwed by mirror plates to, the panelling of a room, or hung from, over, or screwed by mirror plates to, the walls of an unpanelled room*".[431] While the paintings in question were all associated with the Earl of Cadogan's family, they had not been as firmly fixed as in the *Berkley v Poulett* case, and had not been in Savernake Lodge as long as the paintings had been in that case.

Tower Hamlets

This case, involving Tower Hamlets London Borough Council and Bromley London Borough Council, is the clearest recent example of a dispute as to whether or not a work of sculpture became part of the land. aThe dispute involved one statue, made by Henry Moore, called the 'Draped Seated Woman'. In fact, he cast seven of them in the 1950s. By 1961, these had been placed in Cologne, Brussels, Yale University, the

---

430 [2012] EWHC 1024 (Ch).

431 *Berkley v Poulett*, p. 95.

USA, Melbourne and Jerusalem. The one the case concerned, Cast 2, was created in 1968. It has become affectionately known as 'Old Flo'. The sculpture is sizeable, weighing 1,500kg.

It had been purchased by the now defunct London County Council. It was placed near three tower blocks on the recently constructed Stifford Estate in Stepney, now in the London Borough of Tower Hamlets. Tower Hamlets wanted to sell it for funds. The London Borough of Bromley objected, arguing that it was the owner as the successor to the London Residuary Body.

As Norris J noted: "*It should be made clear at the outset that this case is about "ownership". No question of trust law arises. Once ownership is established whichever local authority owns the sculpture may deal with it freely as owner, the rights of ownership being exercised by the relevant constitutional organs of that authority in accordance with whatever democratic direction is given to it.*"[432]

In order to determine that question of ownership, Norris J had to trace its history. The issues as to personal property will be dealt with in the next chapter. This chapter will consider whether 'Old Flo' had become part of the land owned by Tower Hamlets.

The London County Council, in the 1950s, adopted the view that it had a cultural responsibility to encourage the provision of works of art. It had a specific power to do so, under s. 157 of the Local Government Act 1957. In the meantime, the Stifford Estate was completed in the early part of 1961; the three tower blocks were regarded as a prime example of modern architecture. They had been designed without any reference to the inclusion of a particular piece of art, although from an early design stage it had been contemplated that a work of art would be placed somewhere in relation to the development. Henry Moore was approached and agreed to sell the final cast of 'Draped Seated Woman' to the London County Council.

[432] *Tower Hamlets*, §2.

Norris J noted that its reception was not initially warm. One correspondent to the local newspaper commented on it in derogatory terms.

> *"What is this? Is this monstrosity supposed to represent Womanhood? Surely there is something wrong with Art when it deliberately sets out to portray a malformed, ill-proportioned wench as a woman. What does the statue, just off Jamaica Street suggest to the passer by? I see on the mound a heap of metal roughly moulded, it is large and it is ugly. I think of the many Stepney Matrons I have the pleasure of knowing. Does this statue do them justice? No!"*[433]

Norris J held that the statue, originally a chattel, never became part of the realty. He referred to the test in *Elitestone*, and in particular, the test of whether an object has been fixed for the better enjoyment of the object as a chattel, or with a view to effecting a permanent improvement of the freehold.

To Norris J, the fact that the sculpture was an entire object, in and of itself, which be removed without damage, and which was not dependent on a location. As he observed at §17, "*It might adorn or beautify a location, but it was not in any real sense dependant upon that location.*" This led him to conclude that it was a chattel. As he went on to observe, "*the sculpture's power was no greater in Stepney than in Cologne or Melbourne.*" It did not form part of an integral design of the Stifford Estate. This, he held, was consistent with the reasoning in *Berkley v Poulett*. It had not become part of Tower Hamlets' land.

Having reached this conclusion, however, he then went on to consider how it had been dealt with as a chattel. This will be considered in the Chapter 8.

The fact that the beauty of the statue was independent of its location was an important factor in the decision. This suggests that, in another case,

---

[433] *Tower Hamlets,* §13.

an art installation might be site-specific, deriving its artistic power from its surroundings, and hence making it part of the realty as a whole.[434]

The relationship with the test in *Dill*

The relationship between the test endorsed in *Elitestone* and applied in previous and subsequent cases, and the test as set out in *Dill v Secretary of State for Communities and Local Government* ("*Dill*"),[435] is not direct, and care should be applied when attempting to transpose decisions or approaches made in respect of one regime to the other. As set out above, the listed building regime applies to the listing of buildings; it does not extend to chattels. In particular, Lord Carnwath made it clear that the mere fact something had been 'erected' on land was not sufficient to make it a building. Furthermore, the distinction between something becoming 'part and parcel' of the land, and something becoming a fixture but still capable of being removed, is not found in the listed building regime, making a direct comparison complicated.

Lord Carnwath discussed the decision in *Berkley v Poulett,* and, in particular, the relevance of the principle he extracted from it that a thing may be a fixture because it is part of the architectural design.[436] This discussion lends weight to the view adopted by Norris J that it was appropriate to consider the relevance of Old Flo to the design of the Stifford Estate.

Having referred to the real property cases, however, Lord Carnwath then turned to the *Skerritts* test, involving a consideration of size, permanence and degree of physical attachment. He approved the movement away from real property analogies in the listed building context: "*real property concepts are relevant to the extended definition, but there is nothing to import*

[434] Marta Iljadica, 'Is a sculpture "land"? *London Borough of Tower Hamlets v London Borough of Bromley* [2015] EWHC 1954 (Ch)' (2016) The Conveyancer and Property Lawyer 3, 242, p. 244.

[435] [2020] UKSC 20, [2020] 1 WLR 2206.

[436] Ibid, §§40-44.

them into the basic definition of building."[437] As a matter of doctrinal law, this is undoubtedly correct: the question being asked is different, and the test applied in *Dill* reflects the more specific question of whether the urbs became '*buildings*' rather than whether they became part of the land (and then, perhaps, capable of being removed or detached).

Conclusion

There remains confusion as to the correct way to approach the aesthetic scheme or architectural design. Cases such as *Berkley v Poulett* offer support for the view that where objects are lightly attached to the land, but are part of an overall unitary aesthetic scheme, this can count as a factor pointing in the direction of their becoming part of the land. Norris J considered the history of the design of the Stifford Estate in the *Tower Hamlets LBC v Bromley LBC* case. The test of whether an object has been placed for the better enjoyment of it as a chattel, or to improve the land, is completely circular: an ornament that improves the aesthetic of the land is presumably being enjoyed as an object as well, unless it is wholly structural and covered up. As Chris Bevan has noted, "*It is hard to justify why a piece of art that is carefully selected, placed in a public setting to accrue benefits for those on the land as well as the wider public cannot be viewed as falling within a specific design scheme when wall-mounted tapestries in a single room can.*"[438]

It is suggested that the difference lies in the remainder of the building itself, and not the object in question. The Elizabethan room under consideration in *In Re Whaley* was designed around the objects in question. As a consequence, if those objects had been removed and replace with, say, drawings of Queen Elizabeth II, the room itself would have lost its aesthetic unity. On the other hand, if Old Flo was replaced by a statue of *King and Queen,* also by Henry Moore and with several examples cast, it cannot be said that the aesthetic unity of the former Stifford Estate would have been affected. This interpretation is supported by Lord Carnwath's observations in *Dill.* This rationalisation, however,

---

[437] Ibid, §52.

[438] Bevan (2021), p. 12.

relies on an entirely subjective metric. In the same way that *Elitestone* has provided a measure of certainty when it comes to dwellings, a decision of the Supreme Court in this area would potentially bring greater coherence to this vexed issue.

CHAPTER EIGHT

CONVERSION

Introduction

The primary way that English law gives protection to legal title in personal property is through the law of tort.[439] This area was substantially affected, but critically not codified, by the Torts (Interference with Goods) Act 1977 ("the 1977 Act"). Prior to the 1977 Act, there were a number of causes of action with often unclear or opaque scope. The 1977 Act partially reformed this area. Detinue was abolished by s. 2. The law of remedies was clarified by ss. 3, 4 and 5, which gave structure to the alternative claims for delivery up of the property itself and the effect of a judgment for damages alone. The remainder of the 1977 Act provided useful rules in respect of liability to two or more claimants, conversion, and uncollected goods. Notwithstanding this useful reform, this area remains very complex, with three potentially overlapping torts: conversion, trespass to chattels, and reversionary injury.

This chapter will consider conversion. The essence of conversion is in the unlawful appropriation of another's chattel,[440] or the wrongful exclusion of the claimant from the use of possession of their goods.[441] Unlike trespass, which covers direct or wrongful interference with a chattel in the claimant's possession, it also covers an injury to the claimant's right or title in the chattel. An owner out of possession (such as where an owner has loaned out or leased his chattel) cannot recover in either tort, but potentially has an action on the case to recover any actual loss to their reversionary interest. By the 1977 Act, the scope covered by the previous tort of detinue (giving a claimant a right to immediate possession for the

---

[439] Duncan Sheehan, *The Principles of Personal Property Law* (2nd edition, Hart, 2017), p. 183.

[440] *Clerk & Lindsell on Torts* (23rd edition), § 16-02.

[441] Simon Douglas, 'The Nature of Conversion' [2009] Cambridge Law Journal 198, p. 209. In this article, Douglas traces the history of the cause of action from areas of liability where detinue did not provide a remedy.

wrongful detention of their chattel) was almost entirely given over to the tort of conversion.[442]

An action for conversion can take many forms. It includes claims where property is wrongfully taken or received by someone not entitled to do so, when it is wrongfully detained, and when the defendant wrongfully denies access to the chattel by the claimant. It can, therefore, include a delivery by way of sale by a non-owner.

This chapter will consider the following.

(1) The legal test for conversion.

(2) How the test was applied in the *Tower Hamlets* case.

(3) Remedies for conversion.

(4) Norwich Pharmacal orders.

The legal test for conversion

The tort of conversion protects possessory interests, not ownership as such, in goods. All that the claimant needs to establish is that they have a superior possessory interest than the defendant; they do not need to establish that they have absolute ownership of the object. In the seminal case of *Armory v Delamire*, a finder of a jewel was held to be able to maintain an action against a party who had wrongly refused to return it to him: the finder's title, while not that of the true owner, was a possessory interest that was a better relative title than that of the defendant.[443]

---

[442] *Howard E Perry & Co Ltd v British Railways Board* [1980] 1 WLR 1375 at pp. 1380-1381, *per* Megarry VC.

[443] (1721) 1 Strange 505; 93 ER 664.

There is no definition of the tort: instead, it is usually outlined through the operation of the tort through examples of liability for different activities.[444]

In *Kuwait Airways v Iraqi Airways*, the House of Lords set out what remains the leading statement of the test for conversion.[445] The case concerned aircraft which were flown from Kuwait to Iraq following the former's occupation in 1990. Six of those aircraft were then evacuated to Iran, who impounded them. The claimant issued a writ claiming their delivery up. The House of Lords explained the basic features of the tort of conversion.

(1) The essential feature of the tort of conversion is the denial by the defendant of the possessory interest or title of the plaintiff in the goods. When a defendant manifests an assertion of rights or dominion over the goods which is inconsistent with the rights of the claimant, he converts the goods to his own use.

(2) The defendant's conduct must be inconsistent with the rights of the owner (or other party entitled to possession).

(3) The conduct must be deliberate, not accidental.

(4) The conduct must be so extensive an encroachment on the rights of the owner as to exclude him from use and possession of the goods.

(5) It is not necessary for the wrongdoer itself to take the goods from the possession of the owner, although this will often be the case. It is sufficient for the owner to be excluded from possession, or possession is withheld from him, by the wrongdoer.

(6) Whether the owner is excluded from possession may sometimes depend upon whether the wrongdoer exercised dominion over

444 Sheehan, p. 188.

445 [2002] UKHL 19; [2002] 2 AC 883.

the goods. Then the intention with which acts were done may be material.

(7) Mere possession of another's goods without title is not necessarily inconsistent with the rights of the owner. It must be accompanied by an intention to keep the goods. Whether the existence of this intention can properly be inferred depends on the circumstances of the case. A demand and refusal to deliver up the goods are the usual way of proving an intention to keep goods adverse to the owner, but this is not the only way.

Conversion is a strict liability tort: as Lord Diplock noted in *Marfani & Co Ltd v. Midland Bank Ltd,* "The *tort at common law is one of strict liability in which the moral concept of fault in the sense of either knowledge by the doer of an act that it is likely to cause injury, loss or damage to another, or lack of reasonable care to avoid causing injury, loss or damage to another, plays no part.*"[446] It can therefore lie against the innocent purchaser of stolen goods.[447]

The taking must be accompanied by an intention to exercise permanent or temporary dominion, that is a deprivation of possession to such an extent as to be inconsistent with the right of the owner and evidence of an intention to deprive him of that right.[448] A more minor interference might, however, constitute a trespass to that chattel.

Tower Hamlets

In the preceding chapter, it was explained how Norris J determined that 'Old Flo' remained a chattel. Despite this, Tower Hamlets were able to demonstrate that they had ownership of the statue. The ultimate conclusion that Norris J reached was that Tower Hamlets had converted the sculpture and, because of limitation, Bromley's title had been extinguished.

---

[446] [1968] 1 WLR 956, pp. 970-1.

[447] *Hollins v Fowler* (1874-5) LR 7 HL 757.

[448] *Sanderson v Marsden* (1922) 10 Ll L Rep. 467 at p. 472, *per* Atkin LJ.

By 1962, the London County Council had acquired the statue. Under the London Government Act 1963, however, the London County Council was abolished with effect from 1 April 1965. The statute vested in the Greater London Council. The Stifford Estate, which had vested in the Greater London Council, was transferred to Tower Hamlets in July 1985 under the Greater London Council (Transfer of Land and Housing Accommodation) (No.3) Order 1981 SI No. 1981/644, but as Norris J determined, the sculpture remained vested in the Greater London Council. The GLC was, in turn, abolished in 1986, and the sculpture vested in the London Residuary Body. From 1986, Tower Hamlets acted as if it was the owner of the sculpture. Tower Hamlets had not only taken the sculpture for restoration in 1992, it had loaned it out to the Yorkshire Sculpture Park in 1987 and 1996. In fact, by the time of the judgment, it remained at the Yorkshire Sculpture Park on an informal basis.

As Norris J held, Tower Hamlets was acting inconsistently with the general right of dominion of Bromley, inconsistently with Bromley's entitlement to use the sculpture at all times and in all places. He referred to the speech of Lord Nicholls in *Kuwait Airways v Iraqi Airways* at §§ 39 to 43, and that of Lord Steyn at § 119. By ss 2 and 3(2) of the Limitation Act 1980, this conversion by Tower Hamlets had extinguished the title of the owner after six years.

Norris J, in particular, referred to the events of 1997 to 2002. The sculpture had been removed from its site. It had then been loaned contractually to the Yorkshire Sculpture Park. Further restoration work had been carried out. These were all regarded to be assertions of the right of dominion over the sculpture inconsistent with the ownership rights of Bromley.

Bromley's counter-argument was that this was simply 'safeguarding' the sculpture: "*the minimum action taken to preserve the immediate safety of goods by moving them out of harm's way is not an act inconsistent with an owner's rights.*"[449] Norris J rejected this argument, noting that any asportation, or carrying away, of property for the use of the defendant or

[449] Referring to *Fouldes v Willoughby* (1841) 8 M&W 540 where it was held that a simple asportation of a chattel, without any intention of making any further use of it, was not sufficient to establish conversion.

a third person, amounts to a conversion. When Tower Hamlets took the sculpture aware for restoration or for contractual loan, it was not merely moving the sculpture out of harm's way but otherwise permitting the owner to exercise dominion over it.

Remedies

By s. 3(2) of the 1977 Act, there are three possible forms of order in a claim arising out of wrongful interference by a person in possession or control of the goods themselves:

(a) an order for delivery of the goods, and for payment of any consequential damages, or

(b) an order for delivery of the goods, but giving the defendant the alternative of paying damages by reference to the value of the goods, together in either alternative with payment of any consequential damages, or

(c) damages.

By s. 3(3)(b), relief under (a) is discretionary, whereas the claimant may choose between (b) or (c). Usually, delivery up is only ordered where damages are inadequate, and the discretion is exercised sparingly.

It is possible to claim interlocutory relief under s. 4 of the 1977 Act, for an order for the delivery up of goods.

It is also possible to claim an injunction where such a remedy is available, such as a *quia timet* order to prevent the defendant from behaving wrongfully.

When it comes to damages, a claimant can only recover in respect of a loss that has actually been suffered. In *Borders (UK) Ltd & Others v Commissioner of Police of the Metropolis*, Mr Jordan was sued by a number of major book retailers for losses on tens or even hundreds of thousands of new books that had been stolen by shoplifters and which he sold from his market stalls. In calculating compensatory losses, the court did not award damages in respect of the proportion of those books which would not have been sold in any case.[450] Damages are usually assessed by reference to the value of the asset in the market place at the date of conversion. If, therefore, the goods are commercially worthless, this will be reflected in the award of damages.[451]

Norwich Pharmacal orders

It is not always possible to identify the whereabouts or potential defendants in a claim for the delivery up of converted goods or where damages are sought. A *Norwich Pharmacal* order requires a third party who is not, itself, a potential defendant, to give disclosure as to the identity of the wrongdoer. It is different to applications for disclosure under CPR, r31.16 (pre-action disclosure) and CPR, r31.17 (disclosure against non-parties): it fills a lacuna where a potential claimant knows that a wrongdoing has taken place, does not know the identify of the true defendant, but can identify a third party who has become involved in the wrongdoing and who can give the identity of the wrongdoer. A *Norwich Pharmacal* order may be refused if an order under CPR, 31.16 or 31.17 would otherwise be available.[452] The jurisdiction to obtain such an order was confirmed by the House of Lords in *Norwich Pharmacal v Commissioners of Customs & Excise* [1974] AC 133. It was confirmed that, whereas disclosure would not typically lie against a mere witness against whom there is no reasonable cause of action, it was possible to obtain such an order where it was not possible to commence proceedings without disclosure of the information from a person who has become involved (albeit innocently) in the wrongdoing.

To obtain a *Norwich Pharmacal* order, a claimant has to demonstrate that:

---

450 [2005] EWCA Civ 197, §7.

451 *Robot Arenas Ltd v Waterfield* [2010] EWHC 115 (QB), §§28]30 *per* Mr C. Edelman QC (sitting as a Deputy Judge of the Queen's Bench Division). The case concerned the arena for the television series, 'Robot Wars'. While the issue did not arise due to the findings in respect of liability, the set was found to only have scrap value, against which would have to be set the cost of removing and scrapping it.

452 *Mitsui & Co Ltd v Nexen Petroleum UK Ltd* [2005] EWHC 625 (Ch), [2005] 3 All ER 511.

(1) he or she has a good arguable case that a legally recognised wrong had been committed against them;

(2) the defendants were 'mixed up in' the wrongdoing such as to have facilitated it;

(3) the defendants were likely to be able to provide the information necessary to enable the ultimate wrongdoer to be pursued;

(4) requiring disclosure was appropriate and proportionate; and

(5) The order is necessary in the interests of justice, and is not sought for an improper purpose.

The applicant will typically have to give a cross-undertaking in damages.

The use of a *Norwich Pharmacal* order to obtain information about an oil painting was considered in *Hickox v Dickinson*.[453] The claimant had entered into an agreement with a third party who was to act as her agent in the sale of the painting. After the sale, the claimant did not receive the proceeds of sale and never saw the painting again. The agent was a fraudster who was subsequently imprisoned for a number of offences involving sales of artwork. The claimant sought information from the defendants as to the whereabouts of the painting and the identity of the purchaser. The defendants argued that the claimant's application was a fishing expedition. The application was granted. In acting as agent for the unnamed purchaser, the second (but not the first) defendant had facilitated the sale and was clearly mixed up in the transaction that transferred ownership. The art-world custom of not revealing the identity of a private buyer was not absolute: it did not prevent a party complying with a court order made for the purpose of pursuing a wrong.

[453] [2020] EWHC 2520 (Ch).

Conclusion

An action in conversion is the primary way by which the owner of a chattel can seek either delivery up of the chattel itself or compensation for its loss where it has been wrongfully detained. As the decision in *Tower Hamlets* demonstrates, however, it is still subject to the rules as to limitation. A failure to bring a claim in time against the wrongdoer can result in the owner's title being extinguished, leaving the wrongful possessor with the superior title.

The ill-defined nature of conversion can make curatorship problematic. It is not at all unusual for museums and other collections to hold items that they cannot with absolute confidence say that they 'own', with their provenance arising from loans or uncertain gifts. If, however, the museum sells an object on loan, there is the possibility of a claim for damages arising out of conversion. In *R.H. Willis and Son v. British Car Auction Ltd*, Lord Denning observed that, in many cases, the only way for auctioneers or other innocent handlers to protect themselves is through insurance.[454] Even if the museum was able to obtain insurance in respect of a sale, it would still affect its reputation.

The decision in the *Tower Hamlets* case does not even assist the museum seeking to loan out works to other collections. As noted by Janet Ulph, "*In order to serve the public, museums are expected to lend objects from their collections for special exhibitions. They are also expected to repair them where appropriate. Yet, according to the decision in Tower Hamlets, these are acts of conversion. Equally, it is part of good collections management to dispose of unwanted items from collections, giving priority to transfers to other museums and, in particular, accredited museums. Yet it now seems clear that a permanent transfer to another museum would also be an act of conversion by the transferring museum, regardless of the fact that the museum did not intend to deny any rights of a third party that might exist.*"[455]

---

[454] [1978] 1 WLR 438, p. 442.

[455] 'Frozen in time: orphans and uncollected objects in museum collections' (2017) International Journal of Cultural Property, 24(1) 3, p. 16.

The tort of conversion, therefore, is a source of considerable uncertainty in cases where a collection contains items of unclear provenance.

CHAPTER NINE

CONVEYANCE

Introduction

The conveyance of works of art and cultural property involves highly technical areas of the law, both in respect of personal property and real property. This chapter outlines the issues involved, while referring readers to more specialist works.[456]

This chapter will consider the following.

(1) The sale of personal property.

(2) The sale of land.

(3) Sale by auction.

(4) Authenticity of heritage assets.

Sale of personal property

The sale and purchase of art and other objects is subject to the normal law of contract in respect of the sale of goods, including the Sale of Goods Act 1979 and, where applicable, the Consumer Rights Act 2015.

The Sale of Goods Act 1979

The Sale of Goods Act 1979 substantially codifies the private law regime in respect of the sale of goods, including the sale of artwork. It follows the Sale of Goods Act 1893, which replaced the previous common law regime. A contract of sale is defined as a contract by which the seller transfers or agrees to transfer the property in goods to the buyer for a

---

[456] For an overview of the issues involved, see Martin Wilson, *Art Law and the Business of Art* (Edward Elgar, 2019).

money consideration (the price).[457] It does not change the general law as to the capacity to buy and sell.[458] Unlike the statutory regime in respect of the sale of land (considered below), and subject to any other regime in respect of contracting bodies such as companies, corporations or public bodies, a contract of sale can be made in writing or by word of mouth, or even implied by the parties' conduct.[459]

Typically in a contract of sale, the agreement itself will fix the price, but it may also be determined by the course of dealing between the parties; otherwise, it will be a reasonable price.[460]

The Sale of Goods Act 1979 imposes a number of implied terms, which will apply unless a different intention appears from the terms of the contract. The following are especially relevant to sale of art.

(1) By s. 10, stipulations as to time of payment are not of the essence of a contract of sale.

(2) By s. 12, unless the contract provides to the contrary or it can be inferred from its circumstances that there is an intention that the seller should only transfer such title as they or a third party may have, the seller warrants that they have ownership of, and title to sell the item; and that the buyer may enjoy the item without interference and free of encumbrances.

(3) By s. 13, where there is a contract for the sale of goods by description, there is an implied term that the goods will correspond with the description. Where this term is implied, in England and Wales, it will be a condition.

457 Sale of Goods Act 1979, s. 2(1).

458 Sale of Goods Act 1979, s. 3(1).

459 Sale of Goods Act 1979, s. 4(1).

460 Sale of Goods Act 1979, s. 8(1), (2).

Outside of any contractual obligation that the vendor enters into, there is no obligation on the vendor to volunteer information about the item which is being sold.

It is generally the case, however, that the buyer will seek information about the provenance of the item (including some details of its history). The buyer may want some reassurance, as well, as to the condition of the item, unless the vendor does provides an express description.

Property passes from the seller to the buyer at such time as the parties intend it to be transferred: this intention is ascertained from the terms of the contract, the conduct of the parties and the circumstances of the case.[461] Section 18 of the Sale of Goods Act 1979 sets out the rules for ascertaining that intention, which apply unless a different intention applies. In particular, where there is an unconditional contract for the sale of specific goods in a deliverable state the property in the goods passes to the buyer when the contract is made, and it is immaterial whether the time of payment or the time of delivery, or both, be postponed.[462] Risk in respect of the item passes at the same time as title, unless otherwise agreed or where a party is at fault for the delay in delivery and subject to any obligations as bailee or custodier.[463] This is therefore an important provision that can be overlooked, especially when it comes to the risk associated with the art, and the need for insurance against damage, theft or other loss.

A seller may, however, impose terms that limit the passing of title. This can create informal security for payment. Section 19 provides that "*Where there is a contract for the sale of specific goods or where goods are subsequently appropriated to the contract, the seller may, by the terms of the contract or appropriation, reserve the right of disposal of the goods until certain conditions are fulfilled*". The seller, therefore, might prevent title passing through a simple retention of title clause, so that title does not pass until payment.

---

461 Sale of Goods Act 1979, s. 17.

462 Sale of Goods Act 1979, s. 18, Rule 1.

463 Sale of Goods Act 1979, s. 20.

The normal rule in a sale is that a party cannot give title which they do not have, a rule that is captured by the Latin tag *nemo dat quod non habet.* This is given effect by s. 21(1) of the Sale of Goods Act 1979: "*where goods are sold by a person who is not their owner, and who does not sell them under the authority or with the consent of the owner, the buyer acquires no better title to the goods than the seller had, unless the owner of the goods is by his conduct precluded from denying the seller's authority to sell.*" Section 21(1), therefore, preserves the position where the owner of the property may be prevented from deny that the seller has authority to sell the goods, such as by way of agency or estoppel.[464]

Section 21(2) also preserves the Factors Acts. A 'factor' is a type of trader who receives and sells goods, who carries out business in their own name without revealing who their principal is. Most factors fall within the definition of a 'mercantile agent' under the Factors Act 1889: by s. 1(1) of the Factors Act 1889, "*The expression "mercantile agent" shall mean a mercantile agent having in the customary course of his business as such agent authority either to sell goods, or to consign goods for the purpose of sale, or to buy goods, or to raise money on the security of goods*". Section 26(1)(a) of the Sale of Goods Act 1979 defines a mercantile agent as a mercantile agent having the customary course of their business to sell goods. By s. 2(1) of the Factors Act 1889, where a mercantile agent is, with the consent of the owner, in possession of goods, "*any sale, pledge, or other disposition of the goods, made by him when acting in the ordinary course of business of a mercantile agent, shall, subject to the provisions of this Act, be as valid as if he were expressly authorised by the owner of the goods to make the same*". Section 25(1) provides that where a person has bought (or agreed to buy) goods obtains possession of the goods, then the delivery or transfer by that person (or their mercantile agent) of the goods under a sale to a person receiving the same in good faith and without notice of

---

[464] See, for example, *Re London Wines Co Ltd* [1986] PCC 121, where the buyers of wine were told that their bottles had been earmarked for them. In fact, there was no earmarking, so no appropriation of the specific goods had taken place allowing for title to pass. The warehouse company was, however, estopped by their representation as against the purchasers. While this estoppel was ineffective against a bank claiming the bottles under a floating charge, it allowed the claimants to sue the warehouse company in trover (now conversion). See the discussion of estoppel in Duncan Sheehan, *The Principles of Personal Property Law* (2nd edition, Hart, 2017) pp. 56-60.

the rights of the original seller, has the same effect as if the delivery or transfer were a mercantile agent in possession of the goods with the consent of the owner.

Section 25(1) is a complicated provision that can be broken down as follows. The Owner (O) agrees to sell to the Purchaser (P) a painting. P has not yet taken ownership of the painting, but with consent of the Owner, takes possession of the painting. This is relatively common where the sale contract provides that ownership passes on payment (as opposed to delivery). P then sells or by "other disposition" delivers the goods to another person (A) who (i) receives the goods in good faith, and (ii) without notice of the rights of S. Section 25(1) deems that this second disposition has the same effect **as if** P was a mercantile agent in possession of the goods with the consent of the owner. A now has ownership of the painting, even though P never had ownership.

In *Lowther v Harris*, the plaintiff wanted to sell furniture together with a tapestry known as the Aubusson tapestry, consisting of three panels, and another tapestry described as the Leopard tapestry depicting a hunting scene.[465] Colonel Lowther came to an arrangement with Burton Prior, an antique dealer, that he would act as his agent for the disposal of the items. Customers dealt only with Mr Prior, and did not know about Colonel Lowther; but Mr Prior had no authority to complete a sale without the plaintiff's sanction. Mr Prior falsely represented to Colonel Lowther that he had sold the Aubusson tapestry to Corbel Woodhall for £525; in fact, this was a fiction to allow him to get possession of the tapestry, which he took to the defendant, Lionel Harris, who carried on business as an art dealer. Mr Prior sold the tapestry to Mr Harris for a far smaller sum. The Leopard tapestry was simply stolen by Mr Prior and sold to Mr Harris. Mr Harris raised a defence under the Factors Act 1889. Wright J. held that he was a mercantile agent. Mr Prior acquired possession of the Aubusson tapestry in his capacity as a mercantile agent and with the consent of Colonel Lowther, and in the ensuing sale Mr Harris acted in good faith and without notice of Mr Prior's lack of authority: the defence under the Factors Act 1889 was established. On the other hand, Mr Prior never had possession of the Leopard tapestry

465 [1927] 1 KB 393.

with the consent of Colonel Lowther, and so the Factor Act 1889 was not satisfied. Mr Harris was liable to Colonel Lowther in conversion.

The Consumer Rights Act 2015

The Consumer Rights Act 2015 imports a number of modifications in respect of contracts for the sale of goods between a trader and a consumer. A 'trader' is a person acting for purposes relating to that person's trade, business, craft or profession, whether acting personally or through another person acting in the trader's name or on the trader's behalf; a 'consumer' is an individual acting for purposes that are wholly or mainly outside that individual's trade, business, craft or profession.[466] Section 4 preserves, among other provisions, sections 16, 17, 18 and 19 of the Sale of Goods Act 1979, making provision for when ownership of goods is transferred. Section 11 of the Consumer Rights Act 2015 contains the obligation that every contract to supply goods by description is to be treated as including a term that the goods will match the description. Section 17 of the Consumer Rights Act 2015 provides that, save where the contract shows that the trader intends to transfer limited title, every contract to supply goods shall be treated as including a term that the trader has the right to sell or transfer the goods.

One of the major differences between the 1979 Act regime and the 2015 Act regime is that section 12(2) of the Consumer Rights Act 2015 provides that, "*Where regulation 9, 10 or 13 of the Consumer Contracts (Information, Cancellation and Additional Charges) Regulations 2013 (SI 2013/3134) required the trader to provide information to the consumer before the contract became binding, any of that information that was provided by the trader other than information about the goods and mentioned in paragraph (a) of Schedule 1 or 2 to the Regulations (main characteristics of goods) is to be treated as included as a term of the contract.*" The 2013 Regulations make the provision of certain information (such as cancellation rights) to be mandatory in a number of circumstances: this information is therefore given contractual status.

---

[466] Consumer Rights Act 2015, s. 2.

Another important difference is s. 29 of the Consumer Rights Act 2015, which provides that a sales contract is deemed to include a provision that the goods remain at the trader's risk until they come into the physical possession of the consumer or a person identified by the consumer to take possession of the goods, unless the goods are delivered to a carrier who is commissioned by the consumer to deliver the goods, and is not a carrier the trader named as an option for the consumer.

Section 31 of the Consumer Rights Act 2015 then restricts the trader's ability to exclude the operation of a large number of the provisions in the Act, including ss. 11 (goods to be as described), 12 (other pre-contract information), and 29 (passing of risk).

Section 19 of the Consumer Rights Act 2015 broadens the range of remedies open to the consumer. These include rights to reject, to repair or replacement, or to a price reduction. This is alongside existing rights as to damages, specific performance, or termination.

Sale by private treaty

A sale of an object of art often takes place privately, between buyer and seller. This can be carried out directly, or through an agent, such as a dealer. Auction houses increasingly also offer private sale services. A contract for sale might well contain the following terms.

(1) The parties (or, where the parties are acting through agents, confirmation that this is the case).

(2) The price (including any terms as to currency and the risk of currency fluctuation). This may well include provision as to commission. Any relevant sales taxes, such as VAT, need to be considered.

(3) Warranties, including any warranties as to ownership and ability to sell.

(4) Disclaimers of any warranty. The parties may well want to exclude any pre-contractual representations or introduce an

entire agreement clause, so as to achieve certainty as to the basis of the parties' liability to each other.

(5) Condition (including any deemed ability to inspect the article).

(6) Passing of title (including any provision as to retention of title).

(7) Release of the article (such as upon payment).

(8) Transfer of risk.

(9) Any provisions as to authenticity (again, including any disclaimer or exclusion).

(10) Other boilerplate provisions, including confidentiality, insurance, or dispute resolution.

Any sale will also need to take into account considerations as to anti-money laundering, sanctions, bribery, and the relevant taxation regime that may apply, especially where the parties or the article involved are international.

Sale of land

When it comes to the sale of land, the law is especially technical requiring a greater degree of formality, given the importance and permanence of real property.[467] A contract for the sale or other disposition of an interest in land can only be made in writing. Furthermore, it must incorporate all the terms which the parties have expressly agreed in one document.[468] The terms may be incorporated in a document either by being set out in it or by reference to some other document.[469] The document incorporating the terms or, where contracts are exchanged, one of the documents incorporating them (but not necessarily the same one) must

---

[467] See *Ruoff & Roper: Registered Conveyancing* (looseleaf).

[468] Law of Property (Miscellaneous Provisions) Act 1989, s. 2(1).

[469] Law of Property (Miscellaneous Provisions) Act 1989, s. 2(2).

be signed by or on behalf of each party to the contract.[470] These formality rules do not apply to a contract made in the course of a public auction,[471] but it is usual for a detailed legal pack to contain the terms of the sale. An interest in land can only be disposed of except by writing signed by the person creating or conveying the same, or by his agent thereunto lawfully authorised in writing.[472] As for the conveyance of a legal interest in land, it is necessary for this to take place by way of deed.[473]

As was discussed in Chapter 8, a conveyance of land will typically include the buildings and all objects comprising part of the land. If the vendor intends to retain objects which are part of the land (or if there is any uncertainty about their status), they should record the same as a term of the sale agreement and the conveyance.[474] In *Botham v TSB Bank Plc*, the Court of Appeal considered a number of domestic items and their status as to whether they became part of the land or chattel: for example, in that case, ornamental light fittings or chandeliers which were suspended from a ceiling rose were treated as chattels.[475]

The auction

The law of auctions is technical area. What follows is only an overview.[476]

The concept of a public auction is highly efficient: large amounts of property (which can be both real property and personal property) is offered up for sale to the public at large. Rather than negotiating a sale with a buyer by way of private treatise, the property for sale is displayed

---

[470] Law of Property (Miscellaneous Provisions) Act 1989, s. 2(3).

[471] Law of Property (Miscellaneous Provisions) Act 1989, s. 2(5)(b).

[472] Law of Property Act 1925, s. 53(1).

[473] Law of Property Act 1925, s. 52(1).

[474] This is to avoid the kind of dispute seen in *Berkley v Poulett* [1977] 1 EGLR 86.

[475] [1996] EGCS 149, (1997) 73 P & CR D1.

[476] See *Halsbury's Laws of England,* vol. 14 ('Auction'); Brian Harvey and Franklin Meisel, *Auction Law and Practice* (3rd edition, OUP, 2006).

to a number of potential buyers, who are then able to bid on the price of the sale.

The auctioneer acts as agent for the owner of the property. The auctioneer will also assume fiduciary obligations towards the seller, such as a duty to care for the property and to act with skill and care. As towards the buyer, the auctioneer gives an implied warranty of authority to buyers that they have the seller's authority to sell the property in question.

The artwork is consigned by the seller to the auction house. The agreement between seller and auction house for the consignment of the property will typically set out a number of standard terms, including the appointment of the auction house as the seller's exclusive agent, the estimate and reserve (if any), and the date of the sale. The auctioneer is paid a fee, often based upon the amount for which the property is sold.

Typically, the auction will be conducted by way of lots, with potential buyers attending in person or through their nominees to bid. Each lot is typically deemed to be the subject of a separate contract of sale.[477] It is also possible to bid via a written bid or by telephone bidding. Bids can also be conducted over the internet. The terms of sale are set out in the conditions of sale in the sale catalogue. If the bidding does not reach the reserve price, the lot remains unsold.

When the auctioneer's hammer falls, the highest bid is accepted and the contract of sale is entered into.[478]

The sale is an agreement between buyer and seller: as noted above, the auctioneer only acts as agent of the seller, and is not a party to the contract of sale. If the name of the seller is not disclosed (as is common), then the normal rule that the agent will be liable under the contract of sale is displaced by the contrary intention normally set out in the auctioneer's conditions of sale that state that the auctioneer is not the principal but is acting merely as agent.

---

477 Sale of Goods Act 1979, s. 57(1.

478 Sale of Goods Act 1979, s. 57(2).

Depending on the terms of sale, the buyer may have to pay a deposit forthwith or very soon after the auction.

In the case of personal property, the buyer may have to pay the full price within 30 days or less. In the case of real property, the sale will complete on the terms set out in the sale agreement, which may include a term allowing the vendor to bring forward completion.

Authenticity

Part of the service of an auction house may be in confirming the authorship and authenticity of a work of art. This is typically an expression of opinion, supported by recourse to third party expertise and, where appropriate, forensic and scientific investigation.

The duty of care owed by an auction house in respect of authentication was set out in the case of *Thwaytes v Sotheby's*.[479]. The case concerned a painting of the same scene of *The Cardsharps* by the Italian Baroque artist Michelangelo Merisi da Caravaggio. As Rose J describes:

> *"The painting depicts three men grouped round a table, playing cards. On the left side of the painting is a young man (the dupe) dressed in a sumptuous purple velvet doublet, his eyes downcast looking at the two cards he holds in his hand. Slightly behind him and to his left, facing the viewer, is an older bearded man (the old sharp) and opposite the dupe, to the left hand of the old sharp is a young man (the young sharp). The old and young sharps are in league against the dupe. The old sharp is covertly glancing down at the dupe's cards and signalling to the young sharp with the fingers of his right hand what cards the dupe holds. The young sharp leans forward eagerly towards the dupe, his left hand outstretched and resting on the richly patterned rug covering the table. The young sharp's right hand is reaching behind his back where, tucked into the belt of his breeches, two additional cards are concealed, one of which he is removing."*

[479] [2015] EWHC 36 (Ch), [2016] 1 All ER 423.

Mr Thwaytes owned a painting of the same scene, with the same three characters. He entrusted the sale of his painting to the international auction house, Sotheby's. They took the view that the painting was a copy, and was not by Caravaggio. It was sold by Sotheby's for £42,000 and it came into the possession of Sir Denis Mahon, a lifelong Caravaggio scholar of great renown and an experienced collector of Baroque paintings. He carried out extensive investigations and announced that it was an autograph replica of the Cardsharps painted by Caravaggio himself.

Mr Thwaytes brought a claim against Sotheby's in negligence and for breach of contract, alleging that their experts had failed adequately to research the painting. The case therefore concerned the scope of the standard of care owed by Sotheby's to Mr Thwaytes.

The first question was whether Sotheby's came under a more onerous duty of care when they were asked to research the painting. The auction house contended that there was nothing that happened here to impose any greater duty on Sotheby's than it would owe to anyone who consigned a work of art for sale, whereas Mr Thwaytes relied on additional points which he argued put Sotheby's on special inquiry as to the quality and importance of the painting. Rose J dismissed this argument: he held that there was no basis for concluding that where a work is consigned to an auction house for research and assessment rather than for sale, that imposes on the auction house a duty to examine the work more carefully than they need to if it is consigned to them for sale.[480]

As for the general duty of an auction house, Rose J referred to the Court of Appeal decision in *Luxmoore-May v Messenger May Baverstock (a firm)*.[481] That case concerned a provincial auction house and not a leading London house: Slade LJ regarded their standard to be that of 'general practitioners' and not 'specialists', and hence that the standard

[480] Ibid, §68.

[481] [1990] 1 WLR 1009.

of skill and care would be judged accordingly. Slade LJ noted the following about the possibility that a painting might be a 'sleeper':

> *"The valuation of pictures of which the artist is unknown, pre-eminently involves an exercise of opinion and judgment, most particularly in deciding whether an attribution to any particular artist should be made. Since it is not an exact science, the judgment in the very nature of things may be fallible, and may turn out to be wrong. Accordingly, provided that the valuer has done his job honestly and with due diligence, I think that the court should be cautious before convicting him of professional negligence merely because he has failed to be the first to spot a "sleeper" or the potentiality of a "sleeper"… "*[482]

Whereas in *Luxmoore-May* the case concerned a provincial auction house, Sotheby's was, of course, a leading one. Rose J accepted that there was a higher standard of skill and care. Firstly, those who consign their works to a leading auction house can expect that the painting will be assessed by highly qualified people. This included ready access to the opinions and services of art historians at the highest levels of scholarship around the world.[483] Secondly, a leading auction house must give the work consigned to it a proper examination with sufficient time to arrive at a firm view (where possible).[484] Thirdly, it would be much more difficult for a leading auction house to rely on the poor condition of a painting as a reason for failing to notice its potential.

Sotheby's' primary defence was that the quality of the painting was obviously inferior to anything that Caravaggio would have produced. This was accepted by Rose J.[485] Ultimately, the allegation of negligence

---

[482] Ibid, 1020. A 'sleeper' is an article which is a great work which is, in fact, unrecognised and which is sold for less than what its true value would be if it was correctly attributed.

[483] *Thwaytes v Sotheby's*, §76.

[484] Ibid, §77.

[485] Ibid, §106.

was rejected: he held that Sotheby's had not fallen below the standard expected of them.[486]

In a sale by description (such as where the article is described in a catalogue), there is an implied term that the article will correspond with the description save where this is excluded.[487] Typically, the terms and conditions of sale will exclude such an implied term.

A purchaser might have a remedy for misrepresentation, such as under the Misrepresentation Act 1967. Again, establishing negligent misrepresentation under s. 2(1) might well be difficult, depending on the circumstances. If, however, the vendor has made a statement fraudulently (either knowing that the statement is untrue, or reckless as to the truth), the purchaser might have a claim in the tort of deceit.

Conclusion

The law in respect of sale of goods from one party to another is generally straightforward. Complexities arise in respect of exceptions to the *nemo dat* rule. The Sale of Goods Act 1979 is based on the framework of the Sale of Goods Act 1893: the regular use of retention of title provisions had not become common. There are recurrent calls for a Personal Property Security Act to be enacted in England. It remains unlikely, however, that this will be implemented for the foreseeable future.

The main consideration is the limited degree of protection given to the purchaser, and the limited obligations placed on the vendor, in respect of the description of the object concerned. Provided that the vendor does not fraudulently mislead the purchaser, it is open to the vendor to exclude contractually much of its potential liability to the purchaser if, for example, an article does not correspond with its description. The scope for excluding liability for misdescription is, however, much less in the consumer context.

---

486 Ibid, §166.

487 Sale of Goods Act 1979, s. 13(1).

PART THREE

A CASE STUDY

CHAPTER TEN

THE STATUE OF EDWARD COLSTON IN BRISTOL

A flashpoint in the debate about contested heritage has been a bronze statue of Edward Colston, a seventeenth century philanthropist and slave trader which was erected in Victorian times in Bristol. During Black Lives Matters protests on 7 June 2020, the statue was pulled off its plinth by a crowd, daubed with paint and thrown into Bristol harbour. It was subsequently retrieved and is presently on display in a Bristol museum.

It was a dramatic illustration of the political argument about public memorials to historic individuals whose activities are now seen, in various quarters and to various degrees, as being objectionable. It was a prompt for the government's changes to legislation and policy, acknowledged in the written ministerial statement.[488] The Colston statue has also thrown up wider legal issues and a number of cases which have not been fully resolved. This section looks at some of those topics.

Background

Edward Colston (1636-1721) was a Bristol-born merchant and slave trader. He rose to become deputy governor of the Royal African Company which controlled trade with Africa and transported slaves to the Caribbean and the rest of the Americas. Retaining his Bristol links, Colston became a Member of Parliament for the city for a short period. He was a major benefactor of Bristol and was for those reasons a much remembered local figure. The statue was commissioned 170 years after he died, by a local printer and publisher, J.W. Arrowsmith. The bronze statue, and accomplished work, was by John Cassidy and was placed on a Portland stone plinth. The plinth itself commemorates Colston with a

[488] Planning and Heritage Update by Robert Jenrick MP, UIN HCWS 713 (18th January 2021).

prominent plaque, which has a bronze dolphin at each of its four corners. The cost of the statue was raised through public subscription and appeals, although the project seems to have needed a large anonymous donation, possibly from Mr Arrowsmith. The statue was unveiled by the Lord Mayor of Bristol on 13 November 1895.[489]

The statue and plinth were made a listed building at grade II by the Secretary of State in 1977. As part of work for the Bicentenary commemorations of the 1807 Act abolishing the slave trade, the Colston list entry was amended. The principal reasons for listing are given as:

> *"* A handsome statue, erected in the late C19 to commemorate a late C17 figure; the resulting contrast of styles is handled with confidence*
>
> ** The statue is of particular historical interest, the subject being Edward Colston, Bristol's most famous philanthropist, now also noted for his involvement in the slave trade.*
>
> ** Group value with other Bristol memorials: a statue of Edmund Burke, the Cenotaph, and a drinking fountain commemorating the Industrial and Fine Art Exhibition of 1893"*

The statute had been contentious in Bristol for many years because of Colston's involvement with the slave trade. Discussions had included placing a plaque on the plinth explaining Colston's life more fully, but agreement on the wording was not achieved.

In June 2020 there were world-wide protests at the murder of George Floyd, a black man, by a white police officer in Minneapolis, USA. During one demonstration in Bristol, members of the crowd pulled the Colston statue off its plinth with a rope, and after the work was daubed in paint, pushed it into the harbour. As the protest continued, a black

---

489 For Edward Colston and the background to the disputes see the list entry and Edward Colston: Listing Controversy (Professor Antonia Layard, 15th June 2020) and 'Listing Controversy II: Statues, Contested Heritage and the Policy of 'Retain and Explain' (Professor Antonia Layard, 25th January 2021) on the University of Bristol Law Blog.

woman, Jen Reid, climbed onto the plinth, stood up and gave a raised fist salute. A photograph of this became one of the public images of the Bristol protest.

The Colston statue was subsequently removed from the bottom of Bristol harbour, and Bristol City Council formed a History Commission to decide what should be done. Entirely independently, the artist Marc Quinn made a 2.3 metre-high statue of Jen Reid, in her photographed pose, from black resin and steel. The work was entitled *A Surge of Power (Jen Reid) 2020.*

Very early on the morning of 15 July 2020 the Jen Reid statue was placed on the Colston plinth without the agreement of the Council. It was removed by the Council the following day.

The Colston statue is presently on display in a Bristol museum, still bearing the paint and damage from the demonstration.

The future of the statue is not finally resolved, but the saga has prompted two legal proceedings, so far, throwing up a variety of issues.

The listed building consent application for the Jen Reid statute

A local supporter of the Jen Reid statue applied for planning permission and listed building consent for the installation of the work on top of the Colston plinth for a two-year period. Citing tensions in the city and risks of further disturbances, Bristol City Council refused to validate or process the applications. The applicants subsequently appealed against the non-determination.[490]

The Planning Inspector noted that the Colston statue had been unlawfully removed without listed building consent and so must be treated as still being part of the listed building.[491] He considered that the

[490] Appeal references APP/Z0116/W/20/3260461, APP/Z0116/Y/21/3269256. The appeal was determined on 4th August 2021.

[491] Appeal decision, § 12.

statue was "striking and attractive", and the plinth had quality in design and detailing. Consequently the building's:[492]

> *"special architectural and historic interest is therefore focussed partly on the design detailing of the Edward Colston statue and the plinth, and partly on the depiction of a citizen who has been remembered by some for his philanthropic acts in Bristol. As such, its significance is artistic and historic."*

The Jen Reid statue was a 'high-quality, bold portrait statue in black resin', commendable as a piece of statuary.[493] He continued:[494]

> *"However, to my mind the Edward Colston Statue is a fundamental part of the Monument, as the Monument as a whole is in recognition of Edward Colston and would not have been erected otherwise. Therefore, to replace it with a statue of someone else would appreciably undermine the Monument's historic integrity."*

That there was a void at present on the plinth did not assist the case for the Jen Reid statue, as the gap arose from an unlawful removal.[495] Consequently the proposal would harm the significance of the listed building.[496] The Inspector also found harm to the conservation area by eroding the link with Bristol's past.[497] There was though no adverse impacts on the setting of nearby listed buildings.[498]

The Inspector then considered whether public benefits would outweigh the harm. He recognised that black women were under-represented in

---

492 § 16.

493 § 23.

494 § 25.

495 § 28.

496 § 29.

497 § 35.

498 §§ 30 to 34.

civic statuary and the depth of feeling of a proportion of the population against Edward Colston. However:[499]

> *"there is little to substantiate the appellant's contention that the work would make the public realm more inclusive and encourage community cohesion, and it is not supported with firm or decisive evidence. Indeed, I was told that numerous objections were lodged against the Jen Reid Statue on the day it was on the plinth last year. From this it can be assumed that, for whatever reason, there is a portion of the city's population who would not agree with the appellant's contention. Moreover, whilst civic artwork promoting women and/or people of diverse heritage backgrounds may be justified to redress any imbalance that exists in the public domain at large, such artwork could be placed elsewhere and not necessarily on this plinth."*

Planning permission and listed building consent for the Jen Reid statue was refused.

The Inspector did though order the council to pay the unsuccessful appellant's costs of the appeal.[500] There had been no legal basis for the council's conscious decision to not take any action on the applications and there was no substantive evidence that harm would have been caused in the city by proceeding with the applications.[501] In the subsequent appeals the council had not identified any heritage harm being caused, only expressing concern about an effect on the History Commission's work. Consequently the Inspector could not assume that the applications would have been refused so that an appeal would have been necessary.[502] The Council had acted unreasonably and put the applicant to unnecessary expense, so the criteria for a costs award was met.[503]

The criminal damage prosecution

---

[499] § 39.

[500] Costs decisions, also dated 4th August 2021.

[501] § 9.

[502] § 10.

[503] § 12.

Four of the participants in the pulling down of the statue and its dumping in the harbour were subsequently charged with causing criminal damage to the statue. They were acquitted by a jury at a Crown Court trial on 5th January 2022.

Informed comment on the reasons for the decision and their legal standing is a little more difficult. Juries do not give reasons.[504] Any rulings by the judge on the defences which were raised are not available as published transcripts. The directions given by the trial, Judge, the Recorder of Bristol His Honour Judge Blair QC, has been reported on a number of legal blogs.[505] Some of the defences raised have also been reported online.[506]

What has not been considered at such length is the relationship between the listed building legislation and the decision. The legal directions to the jury do not refer to the fact that the statue was a listed building and it is not apparent whether that status was addressed in any other rulings. Further, notwithstanding the centrality of the question of ownership in respect of both the elements of the offence and the defences raised by at

---

504 "The jury is thus potentially a random, uncontrollable force in the criminal justice system owing to its inscrutability and imperviousness to rationality in spite of the efforts of some judges to control or even bully what they perceive as wayward juries." Anthony Musson, 'Lay participation: the paradox of the jury' (2015) Comparative Legal History 3(2), 245, 262.

505 See Catherine Baksi 'R v MILO PONSFORD, SAGE WILLOUGHBY, RHIAN GRAHAM & JAKE SKUSE' (Legal Hackette's Brief, 9 January 2022) < https://legalhackette.com/2022/01/09/r-v-milo-ponsford-sage-willoughby-rhian-graham-jake-skuse/ accessed 18 February 2022.

506 The Secret Barrister, 'Do the verdicts in the trial of the Colston 4 signal something wrong with our jury system? 10 things you should know' (The Secret Barrister, 6 January 2022) < https://thesecretbarrister.com/2022/01/06/do-the-verdicts-in-the-trial-of-the-colston-4-signal-something-wrong-with-our-jury-system-10-things-you-should-know/> accessed 18 February 2022; 'Edward Colston statue toppling trial – Liam Walker represents acquitted defendant' (Doughty Street Chambers website, 5 January 2022) < https://www.doughtystreet.co.uk/news/edward-colston-statue-toppling-trial-liam-walker-represents-acquitted-defendant> accessed 18 February 2022.

least some of the defendants, the property law aspects of the case have also passed largely without comment.

The offence charged was s. 1(1) of the Criminal Damage Act 1971:

> *"A person who without lawful excuse destroys or damages any property belonging to another intending to destroy or damage any such property or being reckless as to whether any such property would be destroyed or damaged shall be guilty of an offence."*

The legal issues raised were whether the defendants had a lawful excuse. The claimed lawful excuses, as allowed by the judge to go before the jury for their decision as to whether they were made out, were

(i) That reasonable force was being used in the prevention of crime.[507] This was said to be on the basis that:

(a) the statue was a display of "*writing, sign or other visible representation which is threatening or abusive*", contrary to the Public Order Act 1985, s. 5(1);

---

507 See the Criminal Law Act 1967, s. 3: "*A person may use such force as is reasonable in the circumstances in the prevention of crime, or in effecting or assisting in the lawful arrest of offenders or suspected offenders or of persons unlawfully at large*"

(b) it was "*indecent matter [that] is publicly displayed*", contrary to the Indecent Displays (Control) Act 1981, s. 1.

(ii) The pulling down was within one identified category of 'lawful excuse' under s. 5 of the Criminal Damage Act 1971:

> "*if at the time of the act or acts alleged to constitute the offence he believed that the person or persons whom he believed to be entitled to consent to the destruction of or damage to the property in question had so consented, or would have so consented to it if he or they had known of the destruction or damage and its circumstances*"

(iii) That conviction would be a disproportionate interference in the defendants' rights of thought, expression and protest under the European Convention on Human Rights, articles 9, 10 and 11.

This chapter considers the relevance of ownership of the statue, and its listed building status, to these defences.

<u>The ownership and trust analysis</u>

In respect of the second line of defence in the criminal proceedings, the case appears to have proceeded on the basis that the statue was held by Bristol City Council on trust for the people of Bristol. Two of the defendants said that they believed that the people of Bristol would have consented to what was done, at the time it was done.

The question of the ownership of the plinth and the statue as a matter of law (as distinct from equity) should be relatively uncontroversial. The Jen Reid appeal decision by the Planning Inspectorate proceeded on the basis that certainly the plinth remained a listed building; the appellant argued that the statue itself was not part of that building, but only on the basis that it had been removed from the plinth for some time.[508] The statue

[508] Appeal Ref: APP/Z0116/W/20/3260461.

had been listed on 4 March 1977.[509] Applying the *Elitestone v Morris*[510] test, as considered in cases such as *Tower Hamlets LBC v Bromley LBC*[511], the statue had become part of the land. In respect of the first limb (method and degree of annexation), the statue was so firmly affixed to the plinth that the cap stone was not separated from it when it was toppled and thrown into Bristol Harbour. As for the second limb, the statue and the plinth formed a unitary aesthetic scheme: the plinth was designed to hold a Colston statue of some design. It is doubtful that the plinth and statue could be said to be part of a unitary design scheme with the wider group of memorials in the park, and it is noteworthy that it was a slightly later addition to the water fountain. Nevertheless, the statue and plinth are far more obviously part of the land than Old Flo in the *Tower Hamlets LBC v Bromley LBC* case.

The owner of the land, therefore, owns the statue (subject to any equitable interest in it). There was some suggestion by the Mayor of Bristol, Marvin Rees, in June 2020 that the question of ownership was "irrelevant" because a decision had been made to display it in a museum.[512] This is wrong for two reasons. First, ownership is control: if the owner was determined to remove the statue then, subject to public law restrictions, it would be able to do so. Unless and until the owner's rights have been extinguished by way of limitation arising from any possible act of conversion, they still have that control: this is a core part of the proprietary rights in that statue. It is certainly no answer to the fate

[509] https://historicengland.org.uk/listing/the-list/list-entry/1202137?section=official-list-entry.

[510] [1997] 1 WLR 687.

[511] [2015] EWHC 1954 (Admin), [2015] LGR 622.

[512] Martin Booth, 'Ownership of Colston's statue still not confirmed' B24/7, (24 June 2020) < https://www.bristol247.com/news-and-features/news/ownership-of-colstons-statue-still-not-confirmed/?utm_source=Bristol24%2F7&utm_campaign=ff5cc3d381-bristol247_newsletter_25.06.20&utm_medium=email&utm_term=0_67a9a4e1bd-ff5cc3d381-38908609&mc_cid=ff5cc3d381&mc_eid=10eb3a98b8> accessed 18 February 2022; cited by Philip Kuhn, 'Who owns Colston?' (Bristol Radical History Group, 11 July 2020) < https://www.brh.org.uk/site/articles/who-owns-colston/> accessed 18 February 2020.

of the plinth. Secondly, it forms an important part of the question of criminal liability for the crime of criminal damage, as discussed below.

There is the argument, which became relevant in the criminal trial, that the statue had been 'gifted to the citizens of Bristol. Philip Kuhn has argued that, "*ownership of the Colston statue passed from the statue committee into the hands of the citizens of Bristol and unless there are documents to prove otherwise the evidence clearly suggests that the ownership of the Colston statue has always resided in the hands of the citizens of Bristol.*"[513] There was, however, no conveyance of the land on which the plinth stands to the 'citizens of Bristol', which would have required particular formalities to be complied with.[514] There is no direct documentary evidence, either, that the statue was given on trust, although Kuhn does note that the representative of the statue committee who handed the statue to the Mayor asked him to accept it "*in trust for the citizens of their ancient city*". Even if this was sufficient to establish certainty of intention (which is doubtful), it is unlikely it could be enforced as a non-charitable purpose trust.[515] For example, an attempt to create a trust '*for the benefit of any or all or some of the inhabitants of the County of West Yorkshire*' failed.[516] It also offends the rule against perpetuities.[517] It is unlikely that the Colston statue committee succeeded in creating a non-charitable purpose trust by way of an oral settlement.

This analysis contradicts the prosecution case, as summarised by HHJ Blair QC, that "*the statue was maintained by Bristol City Council and held in trust on behalf of the people of Bristol.*" This was not directly a live issue for the trial – the defendants did not assert it belonged them, and therefore the element of the offence that it 'belonged to another' was

---

513 Philip Kuhn (ibid).

514 Section 4 of the Statute of Frauds 1677; the part of that section dealing with conveyances of land was only repealed in 1926, by s. 207 and Schedule 7 of the Law of Property Act 1925.

515 *Re Denley's Trust Deed* [1969] 1 Ch 373.

516 *R v District Auditor, Ex p. West Yorkshire MCC* [1986] RVR 24; C. Harpum (1986) 45 CLJ 391.

517 Jamie Glister and James Lee, *Hanbury & Martin: Modern Equity* (22nd edition, Sweet & Maxwell, 2021), § 16-008.

satisfied – but the defendants Rhian Graham and Jake Skuse both argued that they "*honestly believed the statue was owned by the people of Bristol and honestly believed that, had the people of Bristol known of the damage and its circumstances, they would have consented to what was done.*" Of course, neither the defence nor the prosecution had to establish the validity of a trust purportedly created in 1895. But looking into the future of the statue, it is unhelpful for there to be uncertainty as to the proprietary interests in it. Kuhn is undoubtedly right to argue that ownership does matter, even if the precise answer arrived at by him differs from the preceding, tentative, conclusions.

Listed building analysis

The statue of Edward Colston and the Portland stone pedestal on which it stood is listed as a building of special architectural or historic interest under the Planning (Listed Buildings and Conservation Areas) Act 1990 ("the Listed Buildings Act 1990"). By s. 7 of that Act:

> "*Subject to the following provisions of this Act, no person shall execute or cause to be executed any works for the demolition of a listed building or for its alteration or extension in any manner which would affect its character as a building of special architectural or historic interest, unless the works are authorised under section 8.*"

A s. 8 consent is a listed building consent. Subject to a potential defence, a breach of s. 7 is an offence under s. 9. Pulling the statue off the pedestal, throwing it in the harbour and causing physical damage in the process would have affected its special interest. Whilst inelegant, these acts would have been 'works' for the purposes of the Listed Buildings Act 1990 and, in the absence of listed buildings consent, unlawful.. As explained above, the protesters were not charged under the Listed Buildings Act 1990, but instead under the Criminal Damage Act 1971. In one sense that was not surprising. The offence of criminal damage is usually used where another person's property is damaged. Listed building offences tend to be raised against the owner of the listed building who has carried out or authorised the works.

That the statue was (and is) a listed building may, however, have a bearing on the defences raised. Subject to any argument that the works did not affect the special interest of the building, the works required listed building consent which had not been granted. There is no general exception or defence of 'lawful excuse' to a prosecution under s. 9 of the Listed Buildings Act. The available defence, which defendants must prove, is in s. 9(3):

> *"(a) that works to the building were urgently necessary in the interests of safety or health or for the preservation of the building;*
>
> *(b) that it was not practicable to secure safety or health or, as the case may be, the preservation of the building by works of repair or works for affording temporary support or shelter;*
>
> *(c) that the works carried out were limited to the minimum measures immediately necessary; and*
>
> *(d) that notice in writing justifying in detail the carrying out of the works was given to the local planning authority as soon as reasonably practicable."*

That is usually for works to stabilise or reduce a building which is in a dangerous condition, but might cover situations where the emergency services need to force their way into a building. It would not cover the pulling down of the Colston statue. The most imaginative argument would be that safety or health was affected by its presence, but a crowd tearing it down was not likely to help public order. On the basis therefore that the removal was an offence under the Listed Building Act 1990 and there was no available defence under s. 9, where should that have left the criminal damage prosecution?

The case does not appear to have explored whether there could be a lawful excuse for causing damage if the act was unlawful under different provisions. That raises though the question whether the use of reasonable force in the prevention of crime is an exception to the listed building offence. Since urgent works for the purpose of health or safety are permissible under the Listed Buildings Act 1990, it is questionable whether crime prevention can justify material damage to a listed building when persons are not at risk.

The other issue is whether the fact that the statue was listed is relevant to other aspects of the offences allegedly being prevented. For example, is the fact that the statue was listed relevant to the question of whether the statute was a "*visible representation which is threatening or abusive*", contrary to the Public Order Act 1985, s. 5(1)?

That something is of historic or architectural interest, including artistic interest, does not necessarily mean that its display is not criminal, although it might be a pointer against it being an offence. The listing explained that it was of special interest for its artistic qualities, the interest in Colston – including for his involvement in the slave trade – and group value in that location.

That the Secretary of State has considered a statue to be of special architectural or historic interest might be said to be an indicator that the effect of the work is not threatening, abusive or indecent.

The listing prevented the Council from removing the statue without listed building consent. So if its display was a criminal offence then it was one that the Council were being forced to commit. That raises the issue of whether the protesters' defences necessarily involved a contention that the listing decision was unlawful. The validity of a listing can be challenged in a defence to proceedings under the Listed Building Act, see *Dill v Secretary of State for Communities and Local Government*[518] but it is not apparent whether it was in this case.

As for the third defence, the relationship between planning controls and the human right to freedom of expression was considered in the advertising case of *Butler v Derby City Council*[519]. Article 10 rights were not sufficient to allow the display of a banner protesting against a proposed development without first obtaining advertising consent. It might be said, by analogy, that the Convention rights of the protestors

518 [2020] UKSC 20, [2020] 1 WLR 2206.

519 [2006] 1 WLR 1346, [2005] EWHC 2835 (Admin).

did not mean that they could remove the statue without first obtaining the requisite listed building consent.

Conclusion

The issues discussed above all go to the question whether there could, on the facts, have been any legal basis for acquitting the defendants. Jurys are not so bound. Whilst the judicial oath includes "*I will do right to all manner of people after the laws and usages of this realm, without fear or favour, affection or ill will*", jurors do not swear to follow the law. They swear to "*give a true verdict according to the evidence*". Juries can, and very occasionally, do acquit someone because they think that they should not have been prosecuted. In a case relating to a matter of political controversy, that is a political judgement, and so justifies the political debate which has ensued about the verdict.

INDEX

MORE BOOKS BY LAW BRIEF PUBLISHING

A selection of our other titles available now:-

'A Practical Guide to Document Signing and Electronic Signatures for Conveyancers' by Lorraine Richardson
'A Practical Guide to Transgender Law' by Robin Moira White & Nicola Newbegin
'Artificial Intelligence – The Practical Legal Issues (2nd Edition)' by John Buyers
'A Practical Guide to Challenging Sham Marriage Allegations in Immigration Law' by Priya Solanki
'A Practical Guide to New Build Conveyancing' by Paul Sams & Rebecca East
'A Practical Guide to Inherited Wealth on Divorce' by Hayley Trim
'A Practical Guide to Shareholder Disputes in Family Businesses' by Ed Weeks
'A Practical Guide to the Law of Forests in Scotland' by Philip Buchan
'A Practical Guide to Health and Medical Cases in Immigration Law' by Rebecca Chapman & Miranda Butler
'A Practical Guide to Bad Character Evidence for Criminal Practitioners by Aparna Rao
'A Practical Guide to Environmental Enforcement' by Christopher Badger & Stuart Jessop
'A Practical Guide to Hoarding and Mental Health for Housing Lawyers' by Rachel Coyle
'A Practical Guide to Psychiatric Claims in Personal Injury – 2nd Edition' by Liam Ryan
'Stephens on Contractual Indemnities' by Richard Stephens
'A Practical Guide to the EU Succession Regulation' by Richard Frimston
'A Practical Guide to Solicitor and Client Costs – 2nd Edition' by Robin Dunne
'Constructive Dismissal – Practice Pointers and Principles' by Benjimin Burgher

'A Practical Guide to Religion and Belief Discrimination Claims in the Workplace' by Kashif Ali
'A Practical Guide to the Law of Medical Treatment Decisions' by Ben Troke
'Fundamental Dishonesty and QOCS in Personal Injury Proceedings: Law and Practice' by Jake Rowley
'A Practical Guide to the Law in Relation to School Exclusions' by Charlotte Hadfield & Alice de Coverley
'A Practical Guide to Divorce for the Silver Separators' by Karin Walker
'The Right to be Forgotten – The Law and Practical Issues' by Melissa Stock
'A Practical Guide to Planning Law and Rights of Way in National Parks, the Broads and AONBs' by James Maurici QC, James Neill et al
'A Practical Guide to Election Law' by Tom Tabori
'A Practical Guide to the Law in Relation to Surrogacy' by Andrew Powell
'A Practical Guide to Claims Arising from Fatal Accidents – 2nd Edition' by James Patience
'A Practical Guide to the Ownership of Employee Inventions – From Entitlement to Compensation' by James Tumbridge & Ashley Roughton
'A Practical Guide to Asbestos Claims' by Jonathan Owen & Gareth McAloon
'A Practical Guide to Stamp Duty Land Tax in England and Northern Ireland' by Suzanne O'Hara
'A Practical Guide to the Law of Farming Partnerships' by Philip Whitcomb
'Covid-19, Homeworking and the Law – The Essential Guide to Employment and GDPR Issues' by Forbes Solicitors
'Covid-19 and Criminal Law – The Essential Guide' by Ramya Nagesh
'Covid-19 and Family Law in England and Wales – The Essential Guide' by Safda Mahmood
'A Practical Guide to the Law of Unlawful Eviction and Harassment – 2nd Edition' by Stephanie Lovegrove
'Covid-19, Brexit and the Law of Commercial Leases – The Essential Guide' by Mark Shelton
'A Practical Guide to Costs in Personal Injury Claims – 2nd Edition' by Matthew Hoe

'A Practical Guide to the General Data Protection Regulation (GDPR) – 2nd Edition' by Keith Markham
'Ellis on Credit Hire – Sixth Edition' by Aidan Ellis & Tim Kevan
'A Practical Guide to Working with Litigants in Person and McKenzie Friends in Family Cases' by Stuart Barlow
'Protecting Unregistered Brands: A Practical Guide to the Law of Passing Off' by Lorna Brazell
'A Practical Guide to Secondary Liability and Joint Enterprise Post-Jogee' by Joanne Cecil & James Mehigan
'A Practical Guide to the Pre-Action RTA Claims Protocol for Personal Injury Lawyers' by Antonia Ford
'A Practical Guide to Neighbour Disputes and the Law' by Alexander Walsh
'A Practical Guide to Forfeiture of Leases' by Mark Shelton
'A Practical Guide to Coercive Control for Legal Practitioners and Victims' by Rachel Horman
'A Practical Guide to Rights Over Airspace and Subsoil' by Daniel Gatty
'Tackling Disclosure in the Criminal Courts – A Practitioner's Guide' by Narita Bahra QC & Don Ramble
'A Practical Guide to the Law of Driverless Cars – Second Edition' by Alex Glassbrook, Emma Northey & Scarlett Milligan
'A Practical Guide to TOLATA Claims' by Greg Williams
'A Practical Guide to Elderly Law – 2nd Edition' by Justin Patten
'A Practical Guide to the Law of Prescription in Scotland' by Andrew Foyle
'A Practical Guide to the Construction and Rectification of Wills and Trust Instruments' by Edward Hewitt
'A Practical Guide to the Law of Bullying and Harassment in the Workplace' by Philip Hyland
'How to Be a Freelance Solicitor: A Practical Guide to the SRA-Regulated Freelance Solicitor Model' by Paul Bennett
'A Practical Guide to Prison Injury Claims' by Malcolm Johnson
'A Practical Guide to the Small Claims Track - 2nd Edition' by Dominic Bright
'A Practical Guide to Advising Clients at the Police Station' by Colin Stephen McKeown-Beaumont

'A Practical Guide to Antisocial Behaviour Injunctions' by Iain Wightwick
'Practical Mediation: A Guide for Mediators, Advocates, Advisers, Lawyers, and Students in Civil, Commercial, Business, Property, Workplace, and Employment Cases' by Jonathan Dingle with John Sephton
'The Mini-Pupillage Workbook' by David Boyle
'A Practical Guide to Crofting Law' by Brian Inkster
'A Practical Guide to Spousal Maintenance' by Liz Cowell
'A Practical Guide to the Law of Domain Names and Cybersquatting' by Andrew Clemson
'A Practical Guide to the Law of Gender Pay Gap Reporting' by Harini Iyengar
'A Practical Guide to the Rights of Grandparents in Children Proceedings' by Stuart Barlow
'NHS Whistleblowing and the Law' by Joseph England
'Employment Law and the Gig Economy' by Nigel Mackay & Annie Powell
'A Practical Guide to Noise Induced Hearing Loss (NIHL) Claims' by Andrew Mckie, Ian Skeate, Gareth McAloon
'An Introduction to Beauty Negligence Claims – A Practical Guide for the Personal Injury Practitioner' by Greg Almond
'Intercompany Agreements for Transfer Pricing Compliance' by Paul Sutton
'Zen and the Art of Mediation' by Martin Plowman
'A Practical Guide to the SRA Principles, Individual and Law Firm Codes of Conduct 2019 – What Every Law Firm Needs to Know' by Paul Bennett
'A Practical Guide to Adoption for Family Lawyers' by Graham Pegg
'A Practical Guide to Industrial Disease Claims' by Andrew Mckie & Ian Skeate
'A Practical Guide to Redundancy' by Philip Hyland
'A Practical Guide to Vicarious Liability' by Mariel Irvine
'A Practical Guide to Applications for Landlord's Consent and Variation of Leases' by Mark Shelton
'A Practical Guide to Relief from Sanctions Post-Mitchell and Denton' by Peter Causton
'A Practical Guide to Equity Release for Advisors' by Paul Sams
'A Practical Guide to Financial Services Claims' by Chris Hegarty

'The Law of Houses in Multiple Occupation: A Practical Guide to HMO Proceedings' by Julian Hunt
'Occupiers, Highways and Defective Premises Claims: A Practical Guide Post-Jackson – 2nd Edition' by Andrew Mckie
'A Practical Guide to Financial Ombudsman Service Claims' by Adam Temple & Robert Scrivenor
'A Practical Guide to Advising Schools on Employment Law' by Jonathan Holden
'A Practical Guide to Running Housing Disrepair and Cavity Wall Claims: 2nd Edition' by Andrew Mckie & Ian Skeate
'A Practical Guide to Holiday Sickness Claims – 2nd Edition' by Andrew Mckie & Ian Skeate
'Arguments and Tactics for Personal Injury and Clinical Negligence Claims' by Dorian Williams
'A Practical Guide to Drone Law' by Rufus Ballaster, Andrew Firman, Eleanor Clot
'A Practical Guide to Compliance for Personal Injury Firms Working With Claims Management Companies' by Paul Bennett
'RTA Allegations of Fraud in a Post-Jackson Era: The Handbook – 2nd Edition' by Andrew Mckie
'RTA Personal Injury Claims: A Practical Guide Post-Jackson' by Andrew Mckie
'On Experts: CPR35 for Lawyers and Experts' by David Boyle
'An Introduction to Personal Injury Law' by David Boyle
'A Practical Guide to Subtle Brain Injury Claims' by Pankaj Madan

These books and more are available to order online direct from the publisher at www.lawbriefpublishing.com, where you can also read free sample chapters. For any queries, contact us on 0844 587 2383 or mail@lawbriefpublishing.com.

Our books are also usually in stock at www.amazon.co.uk with free next day delivery for Prime members, and at good legal bookshops such as Wildy & Sons.

We are regularly launching new books in our series of practical day-to-day practitioners' guides. Visit our website and join our free newsletter to be kept informed and to receive special offers, free chapters, etc.

You can also follow us on Twitter at www.twitter.com/lawbriefpub.

www.ingramcontent.com/pod-product-compliance
Lightning Source LLC
LaVergne TN
LVHW052312200926
848481LV00002B/538
* 9 7 8 1 9 1 4 6 0 8 2 5 4 *